C000088093

HILARY PARKE is a freelance writer who tries t(as possible out on the Scottish hills, skiing, snow mate mountain wildlife shot with her camera. many of the high mountain ranges of the world riences, including an encounter with a man-e brought a promising career to an end!

She began skiing as a student at Stirling University and, inspired by some memorable snowy winters, decided to write the first Scottish Skiing Handbook after she and her friends had wondered if the many newcomers to the slopes could be helped to maximise their time rather than spend it in queues or falling off tows!

Since, over the last few years, the Scottish snowsports have been revolutionised by the enormous expansion of the skiing areas and the explosion of snowboarding, a new edition of the handbook was called for. Hilary's comment at the end of it is that, 'the research for this edition – which, of course, means trying everywhere out on as many different occasions as possible – has been more fun than ever – a great many people are working together to provide skiers and snowboarders with some of the most exhilarating experiences they'll ever know!'

Hilary now lives in Aberfeldy, Perthshire, where she teaches her own programme of 'Yoga Fitness', based on her studies of many ancient and modern disciplines and therapies. She is also an active member of the Scottish Wildlife Trust and is particularly concerned with the task of achieving an intelligent and workable balance between the interests of habitat conservation and Scottish snowsports.

Ski & Snowboard

SCOTLAND

HILARY PARKE

First Edition 1989
(Scottish Skiing Handbook)
This edition 1998

Details of titles currently available
from Luath are set out on the
final pages of this book.

The paper used in this book is produced from
renewable forests and is chlorine-free.

Printed and bound by Gwasg Dinefwr Press,
Llandybie, Carmarthenshire.

Typeset in 10½ point Rotis.

*This book is produced with the
co-operation of, yet with total
editorial independence from,
The Ski Scotland Marketing Group.*

*SSMG represents the interests of all
companies and individuals who are actively
involved in the promotion of Scottish snowsports.*

© Hilary Parke, 1998

Ski & Snowboard
SCOTLAND

HILARY PARKE

Luath Press Limited
EDINBURGH
www.luath.co.uk

Acknowledgements

I SHOULD LIKE to thank the Ski Scotland Marketing Group, the Scottish National Ski Council, the staff of all the Scottish snowsports centres and the many individuals who became involved for their help and support in amassing a formidable amount of information. Special thanks go to Elma McMenemy, Bruce Crawford, Shona Ballantyne, Andrew Carruthers, Alison Hood, Fiona Grant, Tania Adams and Catriona Scott, all of whom have given much of their valuable time to help bring the text together. I think we would all also like to thank whoever it was who invented the fax machine: without it our task would have been much more onerous!

Hilary Parke
December 1997

Contents

PART TWO

The Scottish Skiing and Snowboarding Centres

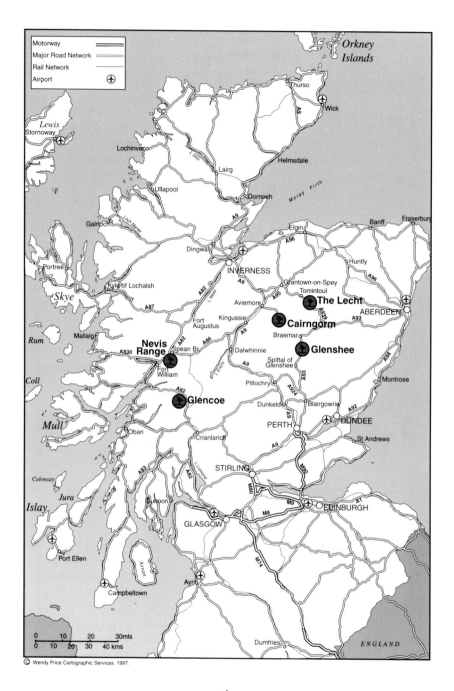

Foreword

I READ THE NEW Ski & Snowboard Scotland Book whilst training for my first World Cup in America. Although thousands of miles from home, the descriptions of the resorts made me feel very close and I giggled as I read about the race trainees barging in front of the lift line.

Reading the book brought back many happy memories of my early training days at the dry slope in Edinburgh and of many brilliant weekends in the Cairngorms.

It took a lot of hard work, determination, and support from those around me to get where I am now but when the results come the hard work seems a small price to pay.

When I look back it seems like ages ago since it was us annoying the coaches and jumping the lift queue but it was all worth it and those were definitely some of my happiest skiing days.

I hope parents reading this book will be inspired to get in touch with some clubs or book their children in for training at the dry slopes: maybe then in the next decade the British Womens team will be bigger than just Shona and myself!

Emma Carrick-Anderson
British Alpine Ski Team
November 1997

INTRODUCTION

SCOTTISH SNOWSPORTS have a character all of their own – and not always in the way you might expect. Contrary to widely-held beliefs, Scottish mountain weather is not consistently arctic in winter. In fact, the number of clear, sunny days is remarkably high and the insulation offered by modern outdoor clothing is excellent: people of all ages and descriptions are out every day of the winter and they nearly all come back for more!

Even on those occasions when the weather is less than perfect it is possible to enjoy an excellent day simply by seeking out the most sheltered runs and making more frequent stops at the mountain restaurants. Ironically, it often seems to be on the least auspicious days, weather-wise, that the skis or board run especially well, that the social climate is at its best and that a sudden weather window appears, giving a stunning view of a vast white amphitheatre of peaks you never suspected exist . . .

. . . or you are the one who discovers, first thing in the morning, a whole corrie of gleaming fresh snow no-one else has found . . .

. . . or, just as you turn for home on the last run of the day, the setting sun colours the ranges orange . . .

I speak, you might have guessed, as an addict, and there are many more who, like me, have found that the skiing and snowboarding to be had in the Scottish mountains is not a poor relative of a foreign winter sports holiday: expertly-groomed pistes, snow-making machines, excellent mountain restaurants and super-efficient uplift make Scottish snowsports an exhilarating experience you want to repeat again and again.

However, whether your interest is downhill skiing, snowboarding or cross-country touring, it takes organisation, effort and money to get the best out of it. The aim of this book is to help everyone maximise what is available, so that the time they spend on the snow is memorable for all the right reasons.

Those of us who have been enjoying Scottish snowsports for a good few years have often discussed the things we know now which we wish we'd known a lot earlier. We wouldn't have been deterred – and would probably have made some of the same mistakes and lived to tell the tale – but we would certainly have spent a lot less time floundering, falling and getting frustrated with lift queues and pistes of a different standard to our skills – and a lot more time thinking, 'Wow – so this is what it's all about!'

"Hey guys — I think we may have missed the green run . . ."

PART ONE

Chapter One

Getting There

FOR THOSE who can think of better ways of spending a morning than staring at a set of closed snow gates, the snow, weather and road reports can save a lot of time, money and frustration.

This is not to suggest that these reports should be regarded as infallible: the most they can do is tell you what conditions were like at the time they were issued, so for this reason it's wise to take note of the report time and go for the most up-to-date service available. After that it's a case of tuning in to the ever-changing weather forecasts, or consulting your crystal ball, whichever you trust most.

It's perfectly normal for the mountain roads to be blocked first thing in the morning and then cleared as a matter of routine. Only when there's been an exceptional snowfall or the blizzard continues to rage on through the morning do real problems arise. If high winds and heavy snowfalls are filling in the roads as fast as they can be cleared, the police may be obliged to keep them closed until the snow-plough crews can get ahead of the situation. Your only consolation on such a day is that the conditions would have been totally filthy even if you had got to the slopes. Chairlifts are unable to run in high winds and often the more exposed tows also have to be stopped.

Hit the road or hit the hay?

All the resorts have their own snow hotline – see summary table overleaf. This provides a pre-recorded message: usually the first message goes out between 7am and 8am, but this may vary according to the prevailing conditions. Remember that in bad weather it may take time for an assessment to be made, especially if it is still

"Wow – so this is what it's all about!"

SNOW CONDITION REPORTS

RESORT	HOTLINE
	(0891 calls cost 50p per minute)
CAIRNGORM TEL: 01479 811000	0891 654 655 or 0891 333 111 with Area code: 655
GLENSHEE TEL: 013397 41628	0891 654 656 or 0891 333 111 with Area code: 656
GLENCOE TEL: 01855 851 232	0891 654 658 or 0891 333 111 with Area code: 658
THE LECHT TEL: 01975 651440	0891 654 657 or 0891 333 111 with Area code: 657
NEVIS RANGE TEL: 01397 705825	0891 654 660 or 0891 333 111 with Area code: 660
CROSS-COUNTRY SKIING	0891 654 661

WEATHER REPORTS

GENERAL: METCALL SKI SCOTLAND	0331 411 200
WEST HIGHLANDS	0891 333 198
EAST HIGHLANDS	0891 333 197

WINTER ROAD WEATHERLINE

AREA	NUMBER
	DIAL 0891 333 111 followed by AREA CODE
HIGHLAND	870
GRAMPIAN	871
CENTRAL/TAYSIDE	872
LOTHIAN/FIFE/BORDERS	873
STRATHCLYDE/DUMFRIES/GALLOWAY	874

"I wouldn't put <u>that</u> on the
recorded message if I were you . . ."

dark. Most resorts update their messages during the day if conditions change significantly, and the majority also put out an end-of-day report which can give you a broad idea of how much snow there is and how much uplift is running. Some resorts also have a fax service.

In addition to the resorts' own hotlines there are commercial snow information services. These are charged at the premium rate. There is a general 'overview' report of conditions and weather at all the resorts, and then there are individual numbers for each resort and for cross-country skiing. You can also get up-to-date information from Ceefax, Teletext and Web pages (see individual centres section).

All the reports can be exceedingly useful provided a few points are heeded. Always note the time of day that the report was issued; if, for instance, it was the previous evening, conditions may have changed drastically overnight, for better or worse. Try to get the most recent information you can, bearing in mind that many of the commercial numbers are charged at hefty rates. Radio, Teletext and fax tend to work out cheaper if you do a lot of snowsports.

Understanding the Lingua-Reporta . . .

Freezing Level. The term 'freezing level' (FL) does not refer to the bits of one's anatomy which feel the cold first. It does, in fact, give clues for assessing snow and weather conditions. The lower the FL, the

Temp Karlich) -2
Snow Level: 2500
Vertical Runs: 1500

"Hey — I told ya not to have
the Tandoori Chicken, man."

longer the runs will keep their snow (or ice) and the colder the air temperature will be. The FL tends to rise during the day, often to well above the summits, accompanied by a corresponding softening of the pistes.

Vertical Runs (VR). Thankfully not a form of skier's dysentery, this refers to the total length of uninterrupted piste available. As you get to know a resort and the lengths of its runs, this figure will give you a good idea of how well the cover is holding. At the end of the season in particular, the VR figure is especially useful: a sudden, substantial reduction in the VR length probably means that one of the main low-level runs has expired from lack of snow.

On the Road . . .

It is an unfortunate fact that snow has the habit of falling not only on the pistes, where it is welcomed joyously, but also on the access roads, where it can cause trouble. The centre managers, who get blamed for most things, have yet to come up with a way of preventing this, but both they and local councils spend a huge amount of time, money and effort in clearing the roads of snow as fast as possible. Contrary to popular myth, the chairlift companies are actually anxious to get people up the hill (so that they can start taking their money from them) but certain combinations of weather and geography can conspire to make this a major task.

After the storm . . .

In the dark and chilly hours, while skiers and snowboarders are still snoring, the snow-clearing squads go to work, routinely wreaking largely unappreciated miracles. On Cairngorm, it has been known for the cutters and blowers to clear a full half-mile of twenty-foot drifts before 10am – and for the team to then face angry skiers demanding to know why the road wasn't open at 8am!

The ultimate success of any snow-clearing operation is a-blowing, literally, in the wind. If the wind is causing the snow to drift back in as fast as it can be cleared, the prospects for the day are depressing. On the other hand, if a storm blows itself out and the wind drops, rapid progress can be made and the slopes opened within an hour or two.

It can be very frustrating to see 'Road Ahead Closed' signs and not to know what the exact situation is. Often, however, everyone else is as much in the dark as you are. No-one, official or otherwise, is in a position to predict exactly when the clearers will battle through. The police, not surprisingly, are reluctant to allow people to hammer on up

"Aye – get yersel' a four-wheel drive,
Cressie – ye dinnae need a' they
fancy snowploughs tae clear the way . . ."

the glens only to get stuck in snowdrifts further along. Most of the access roads have snow gates which will be kept closed until the road is at least passable. It has been known for characters like Big Wullie in his Go-Anywhere four-wheel-drive to try and get round the snow gates "tae ha'e a wee crack at it"; what then happens is that he seriously impedes the snow-clearing process, gets up everyone's nose and hopefully incurs some nasty damage to his shiny paintwork from stones flung by the snowcutter.

On Being Prepared . . .

More often than not the ploughs and blowers win the battle and the impatient hordes are allowed through the snow gates. All then goes well until the inevitable moment when he-who-neglected-to-check-his-treads runs out of traction on a hill. Everything and everyone behind slides to a halt, with or without impact and unkind words, and many find it impossible to get going again. This is the point where those who have spent their hard-earned shekels on four-wheel drive (with or without diff-lock), snow chains, snow clamps or even just studded tyres, will win out, provided there's enough space to get past. Wearing supercilious smiles they steam triumphantly on, leaving the luckless to continue burning their way through the hard-packed snow to the tarmac. However, if Baldy Tyres has succeeded in blocking the road completely (incidentally, he's guaranteed not to have brought a shovel), he will be very lucky not to have his good character besmirched or even his personal well-being seriously threatened. Let no man stand between a snowsporter and his snow.

Freezer on wheels . . .

Every winter the motoring organisations recommend, even to normal mortals, getting the car properly shod and carrying a shovel, a thermos, food and a sleeping bag. And every winter our newspapers feature gripping survival (or non-survival) stories of those who ventured into the wilderness without any of these things and had to be rescued. What most people find hard to comprehend is that their cosy motor car can turn into a deep freeze within a few hours of sub-zero temperatures. In case you do get stuck, keeping the fuel tank topped up is an excellent idea, as you can run the engine intermittently to warm the car. It is vital, however, to check regularly to see that the exhaust pipe hasn't become blocked with snow. There have been several tragic instances of people being asphyxiated by exhaust fumes. The recommended maximum time to run the engine is ten minutes in any hour, in case there are leaks into the passenger compartment, and always check the exhaust is still clear before you start the engine again. You should never go to sleep with the engine running.

The rescue organisations reckon to reach most people within a few hours, depending on daylight and conditions, but you ought to be equipped to survive on your own for at least twenty-four hours. Keeping a permanent stock of energy bars, drinks and a couple of space blankets in the car is the minimum you should do: it might save your life.

To lessen the risk of having to cope with such dramas, check the road situation before you set out, using the numbers above. Local Tourist Information Centres and Police Offices can often provide the most recent information, but everyone should be aware that conditions constantly change.

Keeping a grip . . .

Nowhere is the constant change more noticeable – and dangerous – than on the road surface. Roads which just look wet often have icy patches; roads which appear to have been gritted may not have been, or may have frozen again; dry hard-packed snow can turn to heavy slush in seconds; the outside lane may abruptly cease to exist. Four-wheel drive and anti-lock brakes have contributed hugely to winter road safety but, as with much technology, we tend to over-rely on them. On sheet ice the sheer weight of your vehicle can render ABS powerless to stop you – it may keep you in a straighter line but you'll continue to slide. Four-wheel drive is great for traction and safer cornering, but when a four-wheeler does come unstuck – man, does it come unstuck!

The only safe way to drive in winter is very, very sensitively, with plenty of space all around you, keen anticipation and razor-sharp reactions. (A spin-off of the increasing popularity of mobile phones is that incidents of dangerous driving are often reported to the police so promptly that action against the driver is possible.) On the ski roads especially, where a high proportion of cars contain young children, an attitude of responsibility is essential. The Snow Hog, in his headlong rush to make up half a dozen places in the car park, is a menace at all times but is odds-on favourite to be the first to be caught out by the unexpected. Sadly, when he does buy his ticket to the Great White Piste in the Skies, he may well take some innocent souls with him.

Chapter Two

Into the fray

A space of your own . . .
SNOWSPORTS IN SCOTLAND are expanding at such a phenomenal rate that peak-season parking can be a major problem at the main centres. Roadside parking isn't permitted by the police, for obvious reasons, and it's quite simply the case that, on busy days, latecomers will be turned away. It is important, therefore, to realise that on a sunny day with good snow cover you will be one of many thousands arriving in the first half of the morning; some car parks will be full by 9am on good days, so the moral is: leave home early.

The early bird catches an edge . . .
All the centres now operate half-day tickets, and it is interesting to note that, with the introduction of the morning ticket, a new pattern of centre usage has emerged. Many people now arrive at sparrow fart, disport themselves flat out all morning and leave at lunchtime, while others put in an appearance just as spaces are appearing in the car park around mid-day in order to spend the afternoon on the slopes. Early session freaks tend to be the ones who can cope with the ice and colder conditions better; it's all very well being the first one in the morning to set an edge on, say, Glas Maol, Yellow Belly or the West Wall, but if your skills aren't equal to the hard, unforgiving surface, you may not enjoy it much. Also, with cold muscles, you may be risking an accident.

Timing is everything . . .
Beginners, families and less bold intermediates tend to favour the afternoon sessions as by then the snow has softened, the overhead conditions are often warmer and the slopes will have been pisted, both by machines and people.

Another way to organise the day, favoured by the old timers, is to arrive early enough to grab a space in the car park, take it easy over coffee until the snow softens a bit, ski the lunchtime gap, lunch late and finish the day with a few runs on empty pistes just before the tows close. The essential equipment for this approach is a good book and a thermos flask, for sitting out the hectic spells.

Park and glide . . .

Ski area car parks, being hives of constant activity and incident, make totally compulsive viewing for people-watchers. Many drivers fall into the Testers category. Assuming that the car park attendant must have been selected for his job on the basis of his supreme athletic prowess, they feel they should test his reflexes and are impressed by his ability to leap from under their front wheels with precision timing, without for one moment ceasing to wave his arms about and mouth strange things at them. If they turned down the stereo they would also be impressed by the richness of his vocabulary.

The Fluorescent-Green-Colour-Blind fail to see the car park attendant at all. Possibly they imagine that a man waving his arms about in a car park is just trying to keep warm. These characters just leave the car where it stalls; it then gets in everyone's way and is ultimately shifted by the snowplough.

Meanwhile, their cousins, the Rugged Individualists, seem unable to understand that the whole point of parking in straight lines is to enable the maximum number of cars to get safely in and out – not everyone wishes to stay to the bitter end and starting a third nose-to-tail row is somehow counter-productive.

As all these drivers are an absolute menace, one can only hope they will gradually become extinct.

Erratics . . .

A mysterious phenomenon in car parks, especially at Cairngorm, is the sudden appearance of large rocks which are foreign to the local geology. These are apparently imported to the area by people with suspect hand brakes; the centre staff naturally applaud their caution, as nobody wants cars escaping down the hill. However, when such rocks get buried under the next snowfall, they can have disastrous effects on snow-clearing machines, not to mention the nerves and dentition of their drivers. So, if you do bring your very own pet rock, remember to take it home with you.

On with the show . . .

Once the tricky business of juxtaposing cars is over, and everyone has told everyone else that their lights are still on, and one driver has gone off to have a quiet word with the pillock who cut him up on the access road, the skis and snowboards and boots and poles and clothing start to get unloaded. Since humans are adept at packing first the items they will need first, the whole place quickly begins to resemble a car boot sale. Because everyone is in a tearing hurry to get in their first queue of the day, and because repeated blows to the backside from neighbouring car doors get wearying, the atmosphere of general bonhomie can begin to erode. Wise souls sit and have a cup of coffee whilst the melee sorts itself out, knowing that this is the prime time for playing 'spot the poser'.

"Each individual sport
supports its own style."

Dressed for the hill or dressed to kill?

When it comes to apparel, it is immediately noticeable that each individual snowsport has its own style. Snowboarders as a whole try hard not to look like skiers; Nordic skiers tend to look more like mountain men than piste skiers; old-timers look entirely different from beginners. Yet all items of snowsport clothing and equipment have one thing in common: they are excellent for keeping out the weather. Technology has accelerated improvements in this field: modern materials and designs combine to make outdoor clothing both efficient and attractive and there is now something to suit everyone, and at very reasonable prices. It therefore makes no sense to use fashion garments for snowsports: they are simply not up to the task – and they can be spotted a mile off, too. They are definitely not cool and they're often freezing!

The three W's . . .

So – what do you look for when faced with a bewildering array of colours and fabric types, board and ski graphics, boots and bobble hats?

The most basic rule, whether you're looking for shred threads, piste apparel or wild and woolly wear, is to buy the best clothing you can afford and to take expert advice on which types and brands of hardware to get.

Starting with the threads, whether you're a skier or a rider or a toboggan-pusher, there are three qualities you're looking for and they all begin with 'w':

WATERPROOFING
WINDPROOFING
WARMTH

(1) WATERPROOFING. This is what you will be looking for in your outer garment.

There are two basic types of waterproof garment: those that breathe and those that don't. Go for the breathable option; it will give you many years of good wear, on or off the slopes, and will cost little more than the non-breathable type. The latter is often made from PVC and is fine for gentle pursuits or for being out in a heavy downpour.

It takes very little effort to generate sweat; when this cools, it dramatically reduces the thermal properties of most fabrics and also decreases comfort in a big way! Everyone has heard of Goretex, the breathable membrane which keeps water out but allows sweat to escape. A number of manufacturers use this or similar materials, almost all of which are extremely good. You will find that there are breathable options remarkably low down the price range, including in children's wear, so good protection is affordable for everyone.

15

There is a new generation of water-resistant garments which utilise Activent, a material which allows virtually no moisture to penetrate inwards but has considerably enhanced breathability, making it exceptionally suitable for energetic sports. Because the seams aren't taped, the manufacturers of these garments don't claim they're 100% waterproof, but for the purposes of a day on the slopes, it is likely they would admirably meet most people's needs.

Reading labels carefully, comparing prices and asking the assistant for advice will provide you with the background you need to make your choice.

"He makes me sick —
always showing off his graphics
whenever there's a female around."

Check design . . .

If you should happen to be out on the hill in a snow shower, the white stuff may come in large, sloppy globules, dense flakes, fine penetrating powder or sharp needles, to describe but a few possibilities. To prevent all this from reaching your person, in an outer jacket you should look for: elasticated or very close-fitting cuffs, roomy sleeves, inner snow cuffs, a high, close-fitting neck with a snowproof fastener, a front fastener which has a protective placket to stop water or snow creeping through the zip, a drawcord waist and/or hem, a well-designed hood, preferably with a stiffened top edge and peak, the kind of sleeves which will allow your gloves or mitts to join them without gaps, and a good range of zipped pockets. Salopettes and trousers should have: plenty of room for movement/longjohns, a comfortable waist, not-too-difficult access if you're taken short, the type of hems and cuffs which will marry well with your boots, as much adjustability as possible for wearing with light or heavy layers, and secure pockets for those heady T-shirt days.

(2) **WINDPROOFING**. If your outer garments meet the above criteria, they're likely to be windproof as well, but it's worth checking. On days when you decide to head out in a fleece or sports sweater, it's a very good idea indeed to choose one which has proper windproofing. Most fleeces are just intended to be warm and reasonably windproof, but some have windstopper fabric linings or are made of special laminates which keep out the wind. You can be certain that if they have these properties, the manufacturer will proclaim it on the label. Hats and gloves also come in windproof materials with the advantage of a softer, more pliable texture.

(3) **WARMTH**. Staying warm generally means careful layering. This is an area where modern fibres have revolutionised outdoor sports clothing.

Beginning with the under layer, there are three main types. One is the close-fitting, moisture-wicking vest and long johns, which need to be close-fitting in order to do their work properly. Then there is the looser option which utilises a fabric like Dryflo, used to make baggier T-shirt type vests which are especially favoured by snowboarders. Between these two is a range of garments which use Polartec 100, an excellent insulator and moisture-wicker.

For the next layer, the ubiquitous fleece is the strongest contender. Good quality fleeces are well worth the investment. Some have laminated windproof layers, as described above, while others go for high insulation properties. Many will zip into your waterproof outer jacket, offering greater versatility.

It is worth mentioning here that many of those who do cross-country skiing or other high-energy/high sweat sports swear by the Buffalo system, a single garment which replaces vest, fleece and wind/waterproof. Its manufacturers say that it is best worn next to the skin, and although it doesn't appeal to everyone, it has a staunch band of converts.

Good quality gloves are another worthwhile investment, since cold extremities are the cause of much misery. Most of us find that our hands sweat quite a lot; while you're still warm this is fine, but when you come to put on a pair of damp, chilly gloves or mitts after lunch, it may take a long time for your hands to warm up again. Experienced skiers and boarders take a dry pair of gloves for the afternoon. Another way round the problem is to use silk inner gloves which can be aired at refuelling stops. Those who suffer from Raynaud's syndrome, or simply from cold hands, will be cheered to know you can buy disposable handwarmer packs which provide heat for several hours and can be carried in your pocket. These are especially useful for children – cold hands are usually the first symptom of the 'whining little wimp' syndrome so familiar to snowsporting parents.

Other useful equipment includes a hat or fleecy headband (since much of the body's heat is lost through the head), and securely-fitting, shatterproof sunglasses on a cord. Alternatively, anti-fog goggles with tinted lenses provide good eye protection and improve visibility in mist and snow.

Some of the Scottish centres are extensive, and more confident skiers and riders may spend a good part of the day well away from the car parks and main restaurants. At Glencoe, Cairngorm and Nevis Range especially, many people take a backpack up the hill as they don't want to have to trek all the way down for lunch and then have to get the chairlift or gondola back up again. Therefore, a backpack you can ski comfortably with is useful; these come in a wide range of sizes for carrying what you need, whether it's full survival gear and food for a long tour or just small essentials like lip salve and a litre of Bell's. You may decide to choose a pack with a waist strap to stop it swinging about. This is a good idea, but if crossing a potential avalanche slope, remember always to release the strap. If you're planning to go ski-touring or ski-mountaineering, examine closely the provision for axe, crampon and ski straps, and check that the pack still feels comfortable when fully laden.

The hardware store . . .

Every year from autumn to spring the classified columns in the newspapers sprout an array of ads all telling a similar story. 'Ski boots – latest model – worn once'; 'Snowboard, as new, bargain at . . '. The moral should be clear, that unfortunately it's incredibly easy, in your first flush of enthusiasm for a new sport, to land yourself with the wrong gear. It's also a prime way to lose both money and confidence. There is a huge glut of second-hand equipment on the market, much of it in pristine condition, which is a good indication to anyone starting out that they should hire their equipment until they're hooked. In snowboarding especially, most people make fast progress and a beginner's board may be outgrown in weeks rather than months. Skiers can

also find that a two-week ski holiday brings on their technique so quickly that their skis no longer do what they want. On the other hand, if you try to buy ahead, you won't necessarily have the right board or skis on which to acquire your basic skills, and you may either be put off the sport or just not become very good at it.

At every stage of a sport it's important to have the right equipment. Too many intermediate skiers go for high performance skis, thinking they'll soon grow into them and thus improve their skiing. What usually happens is they find they can't control the skis and, far from improving, go back to defensive skiing. Skis and boards that run too fast for their riders can be a menace on the slopes, too.

Hire and aspire, buy and fly . . .

Many pages could be taken up discussing the relative merits and weaknesses of different boards and skis. However, in a world where technological advances are being made every day, the revolutionising effect of new designs and materials is as profound in the snowsports industry as anywhere else. Here, therefore, are two pieces of advice:

If you're new to the sport, hire first. Learn a bit about your own style and rate of progress and then take advice on what to buy for the next stage. Hire equipment is usually of a good standard, especially at

"What you need, man, is a Heavy Duty Freestyle Bladder."

the start of the season, and hire technicians should be able to fit you out according to your height, weight and experience.

When you decide to buy, research all you can. Buy skiing and boarding magazines and read the latest equipment reviews; find out about sidecut, new bindings, types of boots and the latest construction materials; go to snowsports exhibitions and chat to the traders; visit more than one equipment shop and ask for advice rather than just cruising around looking. If there's no-one experienced enough to answer your questions properly, shop somewhere else.

Getting the gear to the hill . . .

Carrying four or five snowboards or pairs of skis inside a fully-laden car can be uncomfortable, to say the least. This fact frequently doesn't occur to first-timers until they totter out of the hire shop loaded with gear and then realise they've still a good few miles to drive to the car park. Roof bars are available for almost all types of car (and with added fittings are extremely adaptable for many different sports). Roof boxes are popular, as they take lots of clutter, but check before you buy one that you'll be able to reach it easily. Some four-wheel drive vehicles are pretty tall already; one five-foot-nothing lady revealed that she'd been blown off the roof twice while trying to get her skis out of her box. Another warning about roof boxes: in the interests of good taste, remember to take it off if you have to go to a funeral.

A lockable rack is another alternative which also gives peace of mind, since thefts are common, especially from ski centre and hotel car parks. It has been known for boards and skis to be stolen off the roofs of cars whilst the owners were sitting inside lunching. Security locks are worth exploring, too; new designs emerge every couple of years. If you decide to mark your equipment with a UV pen, it's a good idea to add a sticker to the effect that 'this item is marked so it's not worth stealing.'

The hire route . . .

Hiring is justifiably popular, both at the centres themselves and at various places on the way. At peak times and weekends the hire facilities nearest the slopes may be cleaned out fairly quickly, so you need to book in advance to be sure of getting what you need. All Scottish cities and a good many towns, even those some way from the main centres, have hire shops, and you can often pick up the equipment on Friday evening or early Saturday morning. Always make sure you know the opening hours, as running over the time will incur extra charges.

If you've booked lessons with a ski school, you'll find that equipment hire can be built in as part of a money-saving package.

If you're planning several days' skiing or boarding, you may be able to make considerable savings by booking in advance a whole package including hire, tuition, lift pass and accommodation. A number of organisations, hotels and outdoor centres operate such deals: a good way to find out about them is from the Scottish Tourist Board's *Ski Scotland* brochure, available at the start of each season. Local Tourist Information Centres will also be able to supply details of package operators.

When you arrive at the hire shop, if you want to save time you need to be armed with certain items and information:

Money (naturally), or the wherewithal to pay.

A credit card, driving license or bank card, to leave as a deposit – without such security you won't be able to take equipment away.

Suitable socks for wearing under your boots. If in doubt, wear a thin pair and take along a thicker pair. In general, thin ski socks or tubes are best. Some people prefer not to wear socks at all but with hired equipment this isn't a very desirable practice.

Your height and your shoe size.

Your skiing/snowboarding experience.

This list might seem insultingly obvious. However, if you just sit in a hire shop and watch other people, you'll be staggered how the hiring process is made unnecessarily slow by hiccups involving precisely the above points.

The majority of hire shops are well-established and try hard to match the right equipment to their customers; most have staff who are experienced in the sports concerned. However, there are some cowboys about, often of the 'mushroom in the winter, vanish come the thaw' variety, so it's worth conducting a few basic checks before accepting the equipment:

Make sure the metal edges aren't sticking out or badly burred, and that the sole of the ski or board has no really bad gouges. Edges should be reasonably sharp, especially when the reports suggest conditions might be icy, but don't expect them to be like razors; ultra-sharp edges can be more of a liability than an asset.

Watch to see how the technician fits the bindings to your boots. If the bindings seem loose or rickety, draw attention to this and change them if necessary. Ask how to release and reset the binding yourself. It's a lot easier to learn how to do this on the bench than lying on your back in a snowdrift. It's especially important for children to know how to get a ski off if they get it jammed in the snow; often they're to be seen lying like stranded beetles, screaming for someone to rescue them.

Make sure your feet feel comfortable in the boots you're given. Boot technology is now very advanced: it's the feet that cause the problems, so the art is to find the right fit. Your heel shouldn't slide around but your toes should have plenty of room.

Many hire establishments also rent clothing, which is ideal for a last-minute impulse, or if you're not convinced you'll be totally smitten by the sport.

Most people can manage to carry a snowboard, but the first time you pick up skis, you may be struck by the fact that they're not especially easy to carry. Someone near you may be struck by something even more tangible, so increase your snow-cred by taking a few moments to learn how to carry the unwieldy blighters both safely and confidently.

(1) Make sure the skis are held together by the brakes (little bars sticking upwards from the bindings). If they're not, hold the skis with the soles together with one ski higher than the other, then slide the uppermost one down the other until the brakes cross and hold.

"Whaddya mean —
'Cresshead'?"

(2) Take the poles in your left hand (reverse left and right if you're made the other way round), grasp the skis about 15cm above the bindings and pinch them together (trying not to introduce any flesh between the skis as you do so).

(3) Check there's no-one behind you!

(4) Hoist the skis onto your left shoulder and adjust so that they balance nicely.

5) When you feel the skis are really secure, use the hand holding the poles to steady the skis so that you can use the other hand to open doors/ blow your nose/rescue your hat, etc.

(6) Refrain from swinging round suddenly; some people are remarkably humourless when hit on the head. If you want to create a real fuss, try side-swiping some paint off their car.

(7) When you leave boards or skis outside a café or ticket office, always stand them upright so that (a) they don't run away, and (b) people don't fall over them. No-one ever looks where they're going in a ski resort because there are so many fascinating sights to ogle. Boarders are particularly prone to just dropping their boards on the snow, with the result that getting to the café door at busy lunchtimes is like playing chicken on slimy stepping stones. Perhaps it's not surprising that irate skiers have been observed looking around furtively before sending an offending board on its solo journey down the hill.

Chapter Three

'Afore ye go'

UNTIL SOME TIME in the 1970s, the hills were alive to the sound of breaking limbs, notably tibias and femurs. The techno era has brought many advances, especially in boots and bindings, so that snowsports injuries now show entirely different trends. For skiers, strains and sprains, especially of the knees, have largely replaced fractures. In the case of snowboarders, however, one type of fracture is still quite frequent and that is of the wrist, the result of trying to break a fall with the hands. Fingers, hands, wrists, elbows and collar bones are now taking the brunt of falls, and since they were not originally intended for such impact, it's maybe not surprising that more slings and plastered arms and hands are appearing on the après scene.

So how do you prevent this? The unwelcome truth of the matter is that many skiers and riders are not particularly fit or supple; they tend to rush from a week's butt-planting in the office to a weekend's butt-planting on the slopes without realising the physical demands of the latter. Moreover, however fit you may think you are, skiing and boarding use muscles you didn't know you had (and will soon wish you hadn't). Most of us harbour the conviction that we are indestructible and that our innate athleticism is all we need to prepare us. However, the serious side to some of today's injuries is that they don't all heal easily, especially collar bones, and this can have quite long-term effects on quality of life.

Fit to fly?

Pre-slope preparation is something everyone should take seriously. At the start of the season, even regular skiers and boarders take time to get back into their sport again. Those who leap, gibbering with excitement, straight from the car to the chairlift and then plunge down the black run for their first buzz of the day, or, even worse, the season, are asking for it – in the form of pulled ligaments, muscles and tendons at least. Skiing and boarding both demand flexibility, suppleness, muscular endurance, cardio-vascular fitness, eye-body co-ordination, spatial awareness and quick reactions. (Good looks and charm are nice too, but many people get by without.) To assume that we are all naturally

'... who plunge down
the black run for their
first buzz of the day ...'

endowed with these physical qualities is absurd. The best riders and skiers consciously go about finding ways to build up their skills and physique and often the programmes they have devised can be found in books and snowsports magazines. While these make valuable reading, they shouldn't give the impression that a preparation routine has to be complex or incredibly demanding on one's time. Many everyday pursuits and sports can become part of a fitness programme which will not only prepare you for snowsports but will make you feel fitter and better all round.

Below are listed some ideas for activities which will help the various skill-areas for snowsports:

FLEXIBILITY & SUPPLENESS – yoga, stretching exercises, low-impact aerobics, swimming

SPATIAL AWARENESS & EYE-BODY CO-ORDINATION – racquet games, team games, yoga, aerobics

QUICK REACTIONS – team and racquet games, video games, motorsports

ARTIFICIAL SLOPES IN SCOTLAND

ALFORD SKI CENTRE, Greystone Road, Alford, Aberdeen AB3 8JE
Tel: 01975 562380

KAIMHILL SKI SLOPE, Garthdee Road, Aberdeen AB1 7BA
Tel: 01224 311781

GLENMORE LODGE, Aviemore, Inverness-shire PH22 1QU
Tel: 01479 861256

THE AVIEMORE CENTRE, Aviemore, Inverness-shire PH22 1PF
Tel: 01479 810624

THE CRAIGENDARROCH HOTEL & COUNTRY CLUB, Ballater, Royal
Deeside AB35 5XA. Tel: 013397 55858

FIRPARK SKI CENTRE, Tillicoultry, Clackmannanshire FK13 6PL
Tel: 01259 751772

LOCHANHULLY WOODLAND CLUB, Carrbridge, Inverness-shire
PH23 3NA. Tel: 01479 841234

ANCRUM OUTDOOR CENTRE, 10 Ancrum Rd., Dundee DD2 2HZ
Tel: 01382 643735

HILLEND SKI CENTRE, Biggar Rd., Edinburgh EH10 7DU
Tel: 0131 445 4433

BEARSDEN SKI CLUB, The Mound, Stockiemuir Rd, Bearsden,
Glasgow G61 3RS. Tel: 0141 943 1500

GLASGOW SKI CENTRE, Bellahouston Park, 16 Drumbreck Rd.,
Glasgow G41 5BW. Tel: 0141 427 4991/4993

FIFE INSTITUTION OF PE, Viewfield Rd., Glenrothes, Fife KY6 2RA
Tel: 01592 771700

JEDBURGH SPORTS COMPLEX, Jedburgh Grammar School,
Jedburgh, Borders. Tel: 01835 862566

LOCH RANNOCH OUTDOOR CENTRE, Kinloch Rannoch, Perthshire
Ph16 5PS. Tel: 01882 632201

NEWMILNS SKI SLOPE, High Street, Newmilns KA16 9EB
Tel: 01560 322320

POLMONTHILL SKI CENTRE, Polmont, Nr Falkirk, FK2 0YE
Tel: 01324 711660

MUSCULAR ENDURANCE – gym workout, running, cycling, swimming, isometric exercises, aerobics

CARDIO-VASCULAR FITNESS – running, cycling, swimming, aerobics

Many ski magazines have workout programmes to do at home or at the gym, while most gyms and fitness centres have qualified staff who will help you work out a programme designed to target specific muscles. Some gyms have nordic track exercisers and downhill ski trainers, while rolling slopes are found in certain select locations, often connected with a travel company's foreign package sales.

One of the best preparations is to go to an artificial slope during the snow-less months. Some of these are dry slopes, others have artificial snow, and while they can never present you with the full challenge of the hill, they nevertheless allow you to build up physically under more controlled conditions. A brush with the bristles is also a good way to learn for the first time, since it can be done in summer and you can thereby forgo the teeth-chattering pleasure of standing for hours on a blizzard-blasted slope watching your classmates thrashing about in the snow. Practically all the artificial slopes have floodlights, so it's possible to go in the evenings after school or work. It's also said to be more 'challenging' to ski or board on bristles than on real snow; what this actually means is that after weeks of working hard on bristles, when you do finally get out on the snow slopes you find you can perform a whole lot better than you'd imagined, which is very ego-flattering.

When dry-slope skiing, don't take your own skis along unless you're looking for an excuse to buy a new pair. The surface is as harsh on skis as it is on bare skin. A face-plant on the bristles, although rare, will keep you explaining for some time what you've been up to. Definitely no shorts here. Likewise, fingers and thumbs need protecting, so mitts are advisable. Take old ones, as they tend to age rapidly on the tows.

Good for the sole . . .

It's not only the riders who need preparation: to fondly imagine that when you drag your boards or your skis out of the attic in November they'll be ready to go is a touch optimistic. The notion that skis and boards thrive on neglect seems to be widespread but come the first icy morning there's always a stampede to the repair shop to get the edges sharpened.

Unless you're one of those super-efficient people who prepare their equipment for the following season before they put it away, it's likely that not only will your edges need attention but that some P-tex will be needed to fill in the gouges left by last year's most stomach-gripping moments. Our enthusiasm for tackling rocks, heather, peat bogs and snow-fences takes its toll on the sole. If you're keen, you can learn from books and magazines how to do your own P-texing and edges, and some dry ski slopes offer maintenance courses. However, most good equipment shops and hire establishments offer ski maintenance at a reasonable price and have the special tools which enable them to make a good job of it. Some, such as the Cairngorm Ski Hire, for example, offer a special pre-season tuning deal.

If your edges just need a tickle up between services, you can either pop in to the repair shop when you're next near the slopes or buy an edge-sharpening tool. This, used properly, will maintain the right angle on your edges without ruining them and can just take off burrs and give that much-needed extra grip on icy days.

You should also check your bindings for loose screws, worn springs and improper adjustment. If you've bought any second-hand equipment and you're not certain whether it's set up correctly for your weight and height, take it to a professional and get it checked out.

"I don't know — he went to
get his snowboard out of the attic."

"Donald, you know when you
said you'd hot-waxed my
skis for me . . .?"

Waxing seems to be a neglected art these days but the difference a hot waxing makes to performance has to be felt to be believed. Again, it's something you can get done professionally or learn to do at home – but if you choose the latter, you'll find your popularity will plummet if you use the household iron. Not many threads look chic with iron-shaped wax imprints on them.

Once you've honed your skis/board and your body to a state of stunning perfection, you'll start to feel the improvement in your performance and will probably be amazed at how your stamina increases. Watch out, though: accidents and injuries occur when people are getting tired but don't want to stop. (You remember this one from childhood, don't you?) At the end of the day, when the blood is coursing and the spirit is still willing, it pays to be able to recognise when the body is weakening. The best advice I was ever given on this came from a ski instructor renowned for his stamina and daredevilry: 'Never go for 'one last run'; that's the one when you'll get hurt.'

Chapter Four
Uplifting Thoughts

Ticket to ride . . .

NOT EVERYONE IS READY to use the uplift on their first or second skiing or boarding trip, but before long your skills reach the point where trekking back up the slope becomes a pain. This is when you contemplate buying an uplift ticket and, as in any other purchasing operation, it pays to explore the options. There are many types of ticket on offer. They include: full day, full area tickets; half day, full area tickets; full day, limited area tickets; half day, limited area tickets; midweek tickets; weekender tickets; family tickets; beginner's tickets; multiple day tickets; 5-day passes; high season full; low season full . . . confused? So am I. And the offers change from season to season, centre to centre. What it all means, though, is that:

(a) the ski centres are trying very hard to offer their customers a flexible range of options

(b) the only way to get precisely what you want is to phone/fax/send for information from the centres themselves. The chairlift companies issue up-to-date price lists of their ticket options every late summer/autumn and will send these on request (see table of addresses opposite). Also, each autumn the Scottish Tourist Board publishes an excellent guide to all the ski areas detailing accommodation, outdoor centres, courses, ski and snowboard schools, information about the pistes with maps, other activities, eateries . . . definitely a must-have for anyone who plans a trip to the slopes. Called 'Ski Scotland' it is available from travel agents and tourist information centres.

Just the ticket . . .

If you know you are going to be using a certain centre a lot, a season ticket is a good buy. Even in the poorest snow seasons it's unlikely that anyone who is able to go mid-week skiing in addition to weekends will make a loss. Most long-time season ticket holders feel that they've had such good value over the years, it's worth taking the gamble. There are reciprocal arrangements between some ski areas for

SKI AREA ADDRESSES

CAIRNGORM SKI AREA, AVIEMORE,
INVERNESS-SHIRE PH22 1RB
TELEPHONE   01479 861262
FAX   01479 861207
eMAIL   cairngorm@sol.co.uk

GLENSHEE SKI CENTRE, CAIRNWELL, BRAEMAR,
ABERDEENSHIRE AB35 5XU
TELEPHONE   013397 41320
SKI REPORT   013397 41628
FAX   013397 41665

GLENCOE SKI CENTRE, KINGSHOUSE, GLENCOE,
ARGYLL PA39 4HZ
TELEPHONE   01855 851 226
SKI REPORT   01855 851 232
FAX   01855 851 233

NEVIS RANGE, TORLUNDY, FORT WILLIAM,
INVERNESS-SHIRE PH33 6SW
TELEPHONE   01397 705825/705855
FAX   01397 705854
Website   www.ski.scotland.net

LECHT SKI COMPANY LTD, STRATHDON,
ABERDEENSHIRE AB36 8YP
TELEPHONE   019756 51440
FAX   019756 51426

season ticket holders; Glenshee and Glencoe do a joint season ticket, for example, while Nevis Range and Glencoe do special 'Lochaber' deals, and some centres have allowed concessions to season ticket holders from other areas. If you know you're going to buy a season ticket, go for the very worthwhile 'early bird' reduction, which usually means buying it before the beginning of November, but this can vary, so check well in advance. Some centres offer other benefits to their season ticket holders, such as discounts on servicing or tuition, or they put on a special programme of events. Cairngorm also operates a year-round ticket which enables holders to use the chairlift in the summer.

Little bits of wire . . .

When you elect to buy a day ticket you'll discover that you then need to pass a combined IQ and dexterity test before you can get onto the snow, i.e. you have to attach the ticket to your person in the approved manner, using a little squared loop of wire. Usually these are handed over with your ticket, but there's often a box of spare wires on the counter or in a rack.

In theory it's simple: you just slip the wire through the loop of your zip, peel off the backing of the ticket, stick half of it (the ticket, not the backing paper) onto the wire frame, fold the rest under and stick it to itself on the reverse side. See – piece of cake!

What the instructions don't tell you is that the adhesive sticks INSTANTLY to EVERYTHING it touches, like marmalade to a blanket. It will definitely not come off again without self-destructing, so there's no second chance if you mess it up the first time. The point is that it needs to be permanently attached to prevent fraudulent passing of tickets from one person to another.

Ticket Tips . . .

Don't attach it to the very top of your collar; on windy days it flaps in your face and a severely-lacerated chin looks distinctly un-cool.

Because you can't move it from garment to garment, put it on the one you're likely to wear all day. If the weather looks as if it might get hot (it does happen, quite often actually), then attach it to your sweater top or salopettes zip, where you can show it to the lift operator easily while your jacket is on, but be free to take your jacket off later.

Discourage the 'I wanna do it!' child from attaching the ticket him/herself unless you definitely know they're better at it than you. Having to stand in the queue again to beg for a replacement is pretty demoralising.

Upwardly mobile . . .

Using the lifts, especially the draglifts, is an art that has to be acquired. It also demands a certain etiquette. Asking the lift attendant where he went to charm school doesn't guarantee a safe passage up the hill, especially if yours happens to be the fifteenth ski pole with which he's been jabbed in the groin that morning. The vast majority of lift operators are pretty tolerant, which is just as well considering the amount of hassle they get from the ignorant, the inept and the downright rude.

Keeping the tows going is one of the major headaches for all the centres. The lift systems are designed to get the maximum number of users per hour safely up the hill, and when the lifts stop, tempers get frayed.

Mechanical lift failure accounts for only a tiny percentage of all stoppages. The vast majority are caused by the tow users themselves. Even when you see a technician clambering around up a pylon, it's likely that it was a tow-user's misuse that caused the problem. If people took the time to learn a little about how the lifts are meant to operate, it would contribute enormously to smooth running – and more snow-time for everyone.

Chairlifts . . .

There are a number of different designs of chairlift in use in Scotland, ranging from the single, forward-facing chair to the large quad. However, the principles for getting on and off are much the same:

Watch the people in front carefully to see how it's done.

Get your skis/poles/board/backpack sorted out well in advance of your turn.

If you're on your own and it's a multiple chair, look around to see if there's someone who wants to share with you (it could be the start of a beautiful friendship).

When it's your turn, move briskly to the exact spot where the last person got on.

If a skier, align your skis and look behind for the chair coming.

If a rider, watch others or ask how to take your board on this particular chair.

Bend your knees and relax into the seat as it scoops you up.

Put the safety bar down, arranging boards/skis/poles to accommodate it.

Watch for information notices on pylons.

When you see 'safety bar back' or 'prepare to dismount', get your act together.

Stand up as soon as your feet touch the ground – not before, not after.

Head straight down the ramp or step quickly off to the side, depending on circumstances as indicated by the arrows or lift operator.

Get out of the way of the person behind you.

If you have to carry your equipment up or down on the chair-lift, keep it as neat and under control as possible. Clip skis together, remove straps of sticks from wrists, and be ready to raise or remove your backpack if it's too bulky for both of you to fit on the seat. Keep all equipment steady – don't let it drift towards pylons or the top station operator.

Drag lifts . . .

These lifts, which provide a lot more excitement than their name might imply, consist of poma (button) lifts, which take one person, or T-bars, which are designed for two. The techniques for using them are different, so they're described here separately.

What to do with a Poma . . .

Put it between your legs. Yes, really, it's that simple. Or would be, if everyone followed a few basic rules. The trouble is, they don't, which is how all the stoppages occur. So, what's the drill?

(1) If you're a skier, remove the straps of your poles from your wrists and grasp the poles halfway along.

(2) If you're a snowboarder, take your rear foot out of the bindings. Check your board is securely leashed to your front leg. Leashes are compulsory on all Scottish drag lifts.

(3) Wait for the green light. When it shows, seize the first poma in the bundle. If the pomas are tangled, as occasionally happens, untangle them or wait for the lift man to do so. Only the front one will take you anywhere.

(4) Step past the trip bar. This will start your poma off, so flex your knees ready for take-off.

(5) Stand up! Don't sit down on the button! The poles are spring-loaded, so if you sit you'll just end up on the deck. Once you're moving, stand up straight and steer your skis or board straight ahead as the poma pushes you up the hill. Boarders may need to scoot until they get their act together.

(6) If you fall off, let go. This might sound like an insult to anyone's intelligence, but it's astonishing how many people hang on like grim death, shedding skis and clothing as they cut a swathe up the hill. Just let go and try again. If by any chance your clothing gets caught, yell to someone to stop the tow. There are stop buttons on the pylons at regular intervals.

(7) Don't zig-zag. Often you see idiots who think they're cool snaking from side to side; if they do it too close to an upright, they'll pull the cable off the pulley, which puts the tow out of action for ages.

(8) Don't get off before the top. When a bar or rope retracts violently it can easily wrap itself around a pole or the cable, possibly hitting someone in the process. (Not a good place to get hit at the best of times).

(9) Get off where the notice tells you. If you go on any further, you'll trip the safety mechanism meant to stop people being whirled around the top pylon. This will stop the tow dead and an operator will have to go all the way up to reset it. Being an irritatingly common reason for a stoppage, this lowers your popularity rating among fellow snowsporters pretty drastically.

Taming the T-Bar . . .

Although the principle is the same as for the poma, the T-bar, being built for two, is a far more entertaining means of transport – for both user and spectator. Most of the above rules apply but there are extra practical pointers.

" . . . these physically dominant types appear to exist on a diet of garlic and peppermints."

(1) For take-off, stand exactly where the lift operator tells you. Many people creep forward but T-bars were designed to fit just under the butt, not round the back of the neck.

(2) Because T-bars are usually manned, be extra careful not to stab the lift operator with your poles as you take off.

(3) Snowboarders should pair up for T-bars.

(4) If going up on your own (which can be lopsided but safer), do not, repeat NOT, put the bar between your legs. Seemingly intelligent, good-looking guys are seen doing this every season and it makes your eyes water to think about the possible outcome in the event of an accident.

(5) When you get to the top, don't throw the bar away (unless there are specific instructions to do so). British T-bars differ from the continental type in that the rope has to retract fully into the holder before the bar goes back down again, otherwise it can wipe someone out. Therefore, before you reach the top, decide who is going to take the bar. The other person should get off first and ski well away to the side, while the remaining person keeps hold of the bar and lets the rope run right around the wheel at the top. He then lets the remaining bit retract into the holder as it comes past him before letting the bar go and quickly getting right out of the way of the next person coming up. By the time the bar sets off down the hill again it should be back in its holder. Loose T-bars, catapulting around at the end of their ropes, are extremely dangerous. Occasionally a bar doesn't retract properly, even when you've done all the right things, so be prepared to bellow the time-honoured warning, "Mind yer heid!" Non-natives should memorise this phrase, since time spent waiting for a translation might be critical.

You meet all kinds of folk on a T-bar. The Nosey Blighter makes every trip an excuse to probe deep into his or her fellow traveller's psyche, so by the time you reach the top everything about you will be known, even down to the brand of socks you wear. On the other hand, that curse of the slopes, the T-Bore, is determined to make the most of a captive audience and can be quite astonishingly tedious in a very short space of time: he'll have bored the pants off you by the first pylon. The art of shoving someone else off a T-bar whilst staying on yourself is well worth practising, but you should endeavour to make it look like an accident.

You do, however, meet many fascinating characters with whom you can have conversations about the most unlikely subjects. Vivid in

"I don't understand why — it's
bloody uncomfortable."

my own memory are topics ranging from the gruesome-but-fascinat-
ing (courtesy of paramedic, mountaineer and eye surgeon) to the earthy
(sewage processor) and the terrifying (Patagonian explorer).

Conversation is not always possible; sometimes it has to yield to
the more immediate business of staying on the lift. Certain T-bar
companions can prove physically incompatible; large discrepancies in
height and weight may mean a lot of juggling and teetering, but the
one you really need to look out for is the Boot-Hooker. He (or she –
women are adept at this) has the knack of locking his/her boot clips in
a deadly embrace with yours, resulting in a feeling of great instability;
he, being used to it, carries on happily chatting while you launch into
a frantic stamp-shuffle-step routine until you free your boot. You'll
find this is a waste of time, since moments later the boots will be
mating again. All you can do is try to keep your balance and your cool
and hope they'll break apart if and when you reach the top.

The Leaner is sure to be bigger and heavier than you and regards
your role as a supporting one. It is also an eternal mystery why these
physically dominant types appear to exist on a diet of garlic and peppermints. Apart from suffocation, claustrophobia and crushed ribs, your
biggest worry here is hitting a patch of ice, when suddenly your edges
will have to support both of you. If, in spite of all your scrabbling and

scratching, the crunch does come, try to hold on to the bar for a fraction longer than he does, so you can use him as a cushion.

It's easy to overlook the fact that the tows are the most crucial element in downhill snowsports and that without them we'd be back to trudging and herring-boning. Keeping them going and keeping them safe needs to be the concern of everyone, not just the uplift operators. Parents have a particular responsibility to verse their offspring well in both tow survival and tow etiquette.

Queue tips . . .

When you arrive at the slopes, deciding where to start skiing or boarding is a delicate matter. Even the experienced get it wrong quite often, because every piste is different in the way it holds its snow and reacts to each set of weather conditions. An overnight blizzard or a thaw followed by a frost can transform yesterday's dream mogul field into today's nightmare survival course, so you need to approach each day with an open mind.

The fact that there is a long queue for a particular run often leads people to think that this must be where the best conditions are. Known as Sheep's Law, this is usually an erroneous assumption and reveals a basic lack of understanding of human nature.

When released from their cars, snowsporters tend to head straight for their favourite runs, regardless of the snow or weather conditions. Those who are new to the area, or do not yet have a favourite run, then use Sheep's Law to decide where to go. Before you can say, "Please do not scratch my new board", or words to that effect, a queue has formed to rival that at an ice-cream stall in the Sahara.

It is quite astounding how long people are prepared to stand in a queue, often when the waiting time far exceeds the time taken to come down the run. Patience may be a virtue but a bit of enterprise gets you a lot more skiing. The moral is to find a viewpoint and look around. Early in the day may be the time to get right away from the car-park runs and explore the further regions. Then, when the hordes arrive, you can skip off somewhere else.

Unlike some foreign resorts, where the fastest and pushiest get to go up the tows first, in Scotland queuing is a revered art form. The most despised creature on the slopes is the Brazen Queuehopper, easily distinguished by his brass neck and the challenge inscribed on his bandana. He is not to be confused with lesser sub-species such as the Bumbling Twit, who is incapable of working out where the end of the queue is, or the Blind Chancer, who doesn't really care and hopes to slide in unnoticed.

The Brazen Queuehopper relies for success on speed and the element of surprise; he has perfected the knack of arriving smoothly at the front of a line whenever someone is slow to close a gap. Rarely is he challenged but if he is, he'll either pretend to be deaf or claim his pal's been keeping his place. By the time anyone's thought of a response he's on his way up. There is only one way to fettle this creature: with a swift stab of your ski pole or your free foot 'accidentally' release his binding, then fall against him. Having thus incapacitated him, apologise sweetly for your dreadful clumsiness as you push him aside. It's advisable to refrain from practising this trick on ski patrols, chairlift company directors and lift operators, all of whom are permitted to jump queues. It's usually obvious who they are, as they've just emerged from a blether in the tow hut. Lift operators can be slightly more difficult to recognise but look out for unpretentious (oil-stained?) clothing, an expression of world-weariness and exceptional skiing/ boarding ability.

When there is insufficient room for queuing in one line, a second, third and even fourth row may form. This is where most queue-jumping, intentional and unintentional, takes place. Sometimes, as you come down the end of the run, it's hard to decide which is the last line but usually it's marked by someone jumping up and down and shouting, "New queue!" If you pretend not to notice and join an earlier line, you'll find that everyone will just move in on you when you get near the tow and squeeze you out.

If you decide to start a new line yourself, it pays to make an arrangement with the person at the end of the old line, so they can send new arrivals on to you. Select a large, fearless-looking character for this task – it's no good picking a wimp.

Some groups, such as ski school classes and racers, have priority on certain lifts, so if you decide to ski there, you just have to put up with longer queuing times.

Chapter Five

Fun Without Tears

What goes up . . .
A SNOWSPORTS RESORT could be regarded as a giant adventure play-ground. The brochures put out by the centre operators and the tourist organisations foster this image: fun-packed days, snow and sun, every-thing you could possibly need on hand . . . to the point where there is perhaps a danger of the individual handing over all responsibility to the anonymous 'they' who look after you and are accountable for all things. Yet we are not talking about some man-made theme park; we're dealing with the Scottish mountains: majestic, serene and beautiful on the one hand but wild, ferocious and unpredictable on the other. These are the mountains where conditions can turn from summery to arctic in minutes, where you can see for over fifty miles in one direction and under fifty metres in the other.

The companies which run the Scottish ski centres are all too aware of the dangers that can befall anyone who ventures onto the hills in winter. They have all, without exception, gone to great lengths to try to ensure the safety of their customers – rigorously-trained ski patrollers, carefully-delineated boundaries, hotlines to the emergency services, procedures to clear the hill when the weather closes in, a huge amount of expensive snow-clearing and pisting equipment . . . the list is impressive and reassuring. But there is a danger in all of this that we are coming to rely so heavily on others to look after us that we fail to take care for ourselves, and if anything goes wrong we instantly think about suing for damages.

Anyone who has ever studied systems thinking will be able to see where this trend is leading us. Organisations become paranoid about their legal liability, insurance premiums soar, professionals are obses-sively concerned about doing anything which might lay them open to accusations of malpractice. We are rapidly reaching a position where you or I will think twice about stepping forward to help in an emergency. What if I try to help someone who's injured and they die? Might I get sued? In the snowsports world, the mindset which has led to this situation threatens everyone's safety and enjoyment. 'Live now, pay later, let someone else pick up the tab', becomes a subtle, insidious attitude, and on the slopes it leads to accidents.

Putting on a pair of skis or stepping onto a snowboard seems to be psychologically similar to getting behind the wheel of a car, in that it can transform normally decent, caring people into arrogant, cursing, speed freaks. No-one must get in their way or slow them down; they have a right to enjoy themselves.

Many studies have been made of the accidents which occur on the pistes. Over the years certain trends have emerged: that the risk of injury correlates closely to the amount of experience in the sport, that children and young males are the groups most likely to sustain injuries, that males of all ages have more accidents and injuries than females, and that the probability of injury increases with the number of hours skied in a day – the fatigue factor mentioned earlier. But there is one inescapable conclusion on which all the studies are agreed and which is supported by the managers and ski patrols in every area:

SKIING OR SNOWBOARDING OUT OF CONTROL IS THE PRIME CAUSE OF ACCIDENTS.

The quick and the dead . . .

So how do we improve the situation? Although it's tempting to over-simplify and say that it's just because people go too fast, there are particular reasons why this happens. Underlying many accidents is the attitude described above – selfish, impatient and arrogant, but physical factors also contribute. The slope may be steeper or the surface faster than you realised. If you don't or can't put in enough turns to control your speed, things rapidly get out of hand. Your skis or board may not be matched to your level of experience. For example, buying a pair of skis for a more advanced standard than yours is not uncommon at ski shows or in a situation where you don't want to admit you're inexperienced.

It might seem from this that the less experienced skier is most likely to suffer injury from a fall or from colliding with an immovable object. Whilst this is true, some of the worst injuries are the result of collisions between people, at least one of whom has been going too fast. Often the worst offenders are the self-styled experts, too intent on displaying their amazing talents to make allowances for lesser mortals. However, there are always two sides to a story: the situation may be exacerbated by the inexperienced or intermediate skier or boarder venturing onto runs for which they're not yet ready and then getting in the way. The 'expert' gets fed up being impeded and starts cutting through the 'noddies' as he contemptuously calls them. Since the inexperienced are often unpredictable as to where they're going to turn, crashes occur and the results can be severe. Nevertheless, it's

"I think he used to be a waterskier."

THE F.I.S. CODE OF CONDUCT

1. *Respect for others* – A skier/snowboarder must behave in such a way that he does not endanger or prejudice others.
2. *Control of speed* – A skier/snowboarder must remain in control. He must adapt his speed and manner of skiing or riding to his personal ability and to the prevailing conditions of terrain, snow and weather as well as to the density of traffic.
3. *Choice of route* – A person coming from behind must choose his route in such a way that he does not endanger those ahead.
4. *Overtaking* – A skier/snowboarder may overtake another person above or below and to the left or right provided he leaves enough room for the other person to make any voluntary or involuntary movement.
5. *Entering and Starting* – A skier/snowboarder entering a marked run or starting again after stopping must look up and down the run to make sure he can do so without endangering himself or others.
6. *Stopping on the piste* – Unless absolutely necessary a skier/snowboarder must avoid stopping on the piste in narrow places or where visibility is restricted. After a fall in such a place it is important to move clear of the piste as soon as possible.
7. *Climbing & Descending on foot* – Whether climbing or descending on foot a skier/snowboarder must keep to the edge of the piste.
8. *Respect for signs and markings* – A skier/snowboarder must respect all signs and markings.
9. *Assistance* – At accidents every skier/snowboarder is duty bound to assist.
10. *Identification* – Every skier/snowboarder and witness, whether a responsible party or not, must exchange names and addresses following an accident.

always the responsibility of the faster and more experienced skier to resist the urge to show off and give a wide berth to the less competent.

Snowboarders get tired more quickly than skiers, not because they lack stamina but because of the constant muscular demands of riding the board, so they tend to crumple at intervals and remain comatose or seated for a while until they recover. Unfortunately, not everyone is

"Do I look like that girl
in the brochure?"

choosy or even intelligent about where they collapse; this is often in a bottleneck where others come creaming over a rise and find the way blocked by a heap of bodies. Screams, curses, and impact!

Other hazards . . .
It's surprising how often someone skims right through the middle of a ski school class or even a race, which is both rude and dangerous. Anyone who has watched downhill racing on TV knows what speeds the racers get up to; an unexpected arrival on the course at the wrong moment could mean wipeout for both parties. So don't ignore cordons. They're used for a variety of purposes: to keep race tracks clear, to mark steep drops, crevasses and rocks, and to give queuing space for racers on the tows.

SKI & SNOWBOARD SCHOOLS IN SCOTLAND

AVIEMORE SKI SCHOOL, 2 Burnside Rd, Aviemore, Inverness-shire PH22 1SQ. Tel/Fax: 01479 810296

BOARDWISE SNOWBOARDING, 115 Grampian Rd, Aviemore PH22 1RH. Tel: 01479 810336; Fax: 01479 811046

CAIRNGORM SNOWBOARD SCHOOL, Cairngorm, Aviemore PH22 1RB. Tel: 01479 861261; Fax: 01479 861207

CARRBRIDGE SKI SCHOOL, Mafeking, Carrbridge, Inverness-shire PH23 3AS. Tel: 01479 841246; Fax: 01479 841328

ELLIS BRIGHAM SKI SCHOOL, 9/10 Grampian Rd, Aviemore PH22 1RH. Tel: 01479 810175; Fax: 01479 811492

INSH HALL SKI SCHOOL, Kincraig, Inverness-shire PH21 1NU Tel: 01540 651272; Fax: 01540 651208

THE MOUNTAIN SKI SCHOOL, Aviemore, Inverness-shire PH22 1PF Tel: 01479 811707 & 01540 673433; Fax: 01479 811707 & 01540 673303

SCOTTISH NORWEGIAN SKI SCHOOL, 64 Grampian Rd, Aviemore PH22 1PD. Tel: 01479 810656(D)/872309(E); Telex: 01479 873415

SPORTHAUS SKI SCHOOL, Sporthaus Building, Grampian Rd, Aviemore PH22 1RT. Tel: 01479 810655; Fax: 01479 810908

LECHT SKI /SNOWBOARD SCHOOL, Strathdon, Aberdeenshire AB36 8YP. Tel: 01975 651440; Fax: 01975 651426

GLENCOE SKI/SNOWBOARD SCHOOL, Kingshouse, Glencoe, Argyll PA39 4HZ. Tel: 01855 851226; Fax: 01855 851233

CAIRNWELL SKI/SNOWBOARD SCHOOL, Gulabin Lodge, Glenshee PH10 7QE. Tel/Fax: 01250 885255/6

GLENSHEE SKI SCHOOL, Cairdsport, Spittal, By Blairgowrie, Perthshire PH10 7QE. Tel: 01250 885216; Fax: 01250 885212

GLENSHEE SKI CENTRE SKI SCHOOL, Cairnwell, Braemar, Aberdeenshire AB35 5XU. Tel: 013397 41320; Fax: 013397 41665

NEVIS RANGE SKI/SNOWBOARD SCHOOL, Torlundy, Fort William PH33 6SW. Tel: 01397 705825; Fax: 01397 705854

If you are unfortunate enough to have an accident or you come across one, one of the first things you should do (after checking for vital signs and carrying out any emergency first aid, of course) is to stick a pair of crossed ski poles into the snow uphill of the casualty. This acts as a signal to alert the ski patrol and it keeps other piste users from crashing into you. Although we are used to having road accidents rapidly reported by mobile phone, bear in mind that in the mountains there are many places where a signal is unobtainable and less advanced communication methods may be required, e.g. sending someone off to get help at the nearest tow operator's hut.

Many accidents caused by inexperienced skiers could be avoided if more people took lessons before launching themselves onto the pistes. It is an extraordinary fact that people beginning just about any other sport for the first time take tuition as a matter of course, but every day on the pistes the snow is littered with the prone forms of those who seem to think that skiing and snowboarding should come naturally.

The dog hazard . . .

Skiing with a dog may seem at first a nice idea, good both for exercising the dog and enhancing the image of the owner, but dogs are not welcome on the slopes for a number of wholly valid reasons. One is the many inexperienced skiers around who can't stop quickly or take avoiding action when a dog trips over a compelling smell and slams on its brakes. Dogs run over by skis or boards can sustain pretty unpleasant injuries. In certain snow conditions they can also suffer badly cut feet when ice crystals freeze into sharp balls in their pads. Sadly, also, dogs have been known to have heart attacks brought on by the effort and stress of trying to keep up with their owners in heavy snow. Dogs cover many more times the ground than their owners do, so a day's snowsporting must place great strain on them.

Babies, toddlers and children . . .

A great many ski centres throughout Europe and the USA now ban people from carrying babies in backpacks after cases where babies have frozen to death or had to have feet amputated after frostbite set in. A child in a backpack has no means of stimulating its own circulation by movement. Babies are also very vulnerable to injury in the case of a collision, since however proficient the parents are, they may be run into by someone less competent.

Toddlers can start skiing almost as soon as they can walk, but they must proper boots and bindings. Many hire shops have small sizes, and second-hand equipment for children is ideal when they grow out of things so fast. To protect vulnerable small heads from injury most parents obtain ski helmets for their children.

The golden rule with the very young is to make it fun and never push them into doing things they don't want to do. An hour or two on the snow is the absolute maximum at the beginning and even less if the weather is at all unpleasant. Some children are tougher than others, but at the first hint of mutiny pack it in and buy them a hot chocolate. Don't worry if they're a bit wimpish at first; before long they'll be hurtling past you. Booking them into the snow crèche or junior ski school for part of the day allows parents time to ski on their own, while membership of the Scottish Ski Club entitles you to use the mountain huts at Cairngorm, Glencoe and Glenshee, which are excellent refuges especially if the weather changes.

Ski clothing for kids has become just as good as that for adults, with breathable waterproofs and mini-fleeces widely available. It is important to make sure they don't get cold or they'll be put off for a long time. Spare mitts, hat and goggles are essential, while a balaclava for sudden snow storms or wind-blown ice particles is an excellent idea.

If you are taking a young child up a tow, the easiest way is for you to take their poles, set them astride your leg and let them hold onto the bar. Instruct them properly in all the do's and don'ts of tow handling before you let them tackle pomas or T-bars on their own. Single chairlifts often have a lower age limit, usually eight years, while on the bigger chairlifts the responsibility lies with the parent to see that the child is secure and the safety bar is used properly.

Once children become confident on skis they may want to start racing. Race training frequently begins with getting involved in club races, so if you want to raise a ski prodigy, this is where to start.

Reading the conditions . . .

A primary characteristic of Scottish skiing is its variety. It's rare for two days to be alike in snow and weather conditions, and even in the course of one day you can have thick mist in the morning, hot sunshine at noon and be caught in a howling blizzard by four. Sometimes the chairlift companies come under fire for running tows when the weather is bad, but it should be remembered that some of us are tougher than others and there are people who actually enjoy skiing in adverse conditions because it taxes their skills. If you don't want your skills taxed, don't go.

Although the Scots don't have as many names for snow types as the Inuit, weather which comes from the frozen Siberian wastes one day and the Atlantic the next makes it possible to experience such assorted delights as powder, sugar, porridge, wind slab, breakable crust, crud, slush, sheet ice, gnarled ice and even perfect, dry snow – all in a matter of days!

The annual build-up of the snow fields in Scotland is an intriguing phenomenon. The first winter falls are often heavy, with storm-force winds driving the snow into every leeward corrie, burn, gully and depression on the landscape to a depth sometimes of several metres. It is at this point that it is also meant to fill the gaps between the strategically-placed snowfences, but all depends on the speed of the wind and its direction.

Savage thaws may then follow, accompanied by heavy rain, leaving only the gullies snow-filled. Snowsporters and uplift companies then pray for a frosty spell so that the base will harden before the whole cycle is repeated. On the weather charts, depression follows depression, front after front, until hopefully there is a build-up of solid granular snowfields. When well-established, these can resist the warmth of spring until June and even later in the high corries. (There have been years when I and many others have managed to find snow to ski on during every month of the year.) The excellent type of snow known as spring snow is a product of a rapid freeze/thaw cycle. Rain drains quickly through the large crystals, smoothing their edges to give fast, non-sticking snow which demands a more refined technique than the standard 'up, down'. Skiers and riders who equip themselves, both physically and mentally, to meet these conditions, are in for a great time.

As for restricting your snowsports to the days when conditions are good, many Scottish skiers feel that it's far better to wonder at, enjoy and learn from the power of the elements than to experience only the perfect days. As Tom Paul, former general manager at Cairngorm, once said, "The Scots are a breed apart and the Scottish skiing industry is based on their enthusiasm. Here the lifts are modified to run under adverse conditions and they only close if there's danger to the skier or the installation . . . it's up to the individual to make the decision whether to ski or not."

The following section is not to scare you out of ever going skiing again but to give advance warning of what can happen, so that you are prepared and know how to react.

Evacuation procedure

When the decision is taken to close a ski centre, you can be certain there is an extremely good reason. At all the centres the hill is cleared by sounding a siren; if you hear it, you should make your way back to the car park immediately. Chancers who ignore the sirens and try to grab a bit more time will soon find the lifts closed, outermost ones first. When you reach your car, pack away your gear and then wait inside your vehicle for the police or staff to advise you of the evacuation procedure. It's important to wait for this rather than head off willy-nilly, since the access roads may be filling in fast with snow and the safest way to travel is to make up convoys behind the snowploughs. Staff at Glenshee still have mixed memories of playing host to over 2,000 skiers who became trapped at the centre in a blizzard, while I recall the normal 40-minute journey from Spittal of Glenshee to Blairgowrie once taking me a lonely and tense four hours in a slithering four-wheel drive. The moral support of a convoy would have been very welcome.

Scotch mist . . .

What is euphemistically termed 'low cloud' in the weather report may, in fact, turn into something a lot scarier on the mountain tops. When the light goes flat, all the bumps and hollows in the snow become invisible, which leads to severe strain on your personal shock-absorbers, wherever they happen to be located. Yellow-lensed goggles are supposed to help in these conditions and some say they do while others claim they're useless. The only way to proceed is slowly; distances are deceptive in such conditions, sounds are muffled and it may take quite a while to get safely down.

Even more unnerving is being overtaken by a white-out, when you're suddenly enveloped by a shroud of total whiteness which takes away, quite literally, all your senses. No sight, no sound, no sensation of movement – nothing. The feeling of isolation is abrupt and can be disturbing. The most dangerous aspect is that you may well be moving when you think you're standing still, so the first thing to do is to take off your skis or snowboard. If you don't, and other people come into view around you, you may become mesmerised by the movement. It's as if everything is spinning round and round and the poor befuddled senses simply can't handle it. The risk of hitting a boulder, a fence or even going over a steep drop is frighteningly high. The only way out is to walk slowly downhill until you find a recognisable landmark, like a snowfence. If you find a fence, stay inside it – it may be an outer boundary. Keep listening for the sound of tows or other people – but don't assume the latter know where they're going. In the days before Glenshee was so well fenced, large parties of skiers on their way to Butcharts from Carn Aosda often trustingly followed each other on unscheduled tours all the way over to Loch Vrotachan and had to be fetched back by the ski patrols.

If you get really lost in such conditions, there is a golden rule: go down the hill, never up. A feature of all the major ski centres is that, provided you stay within the fences and markers, by going downhill you will eventually get out onto a road or track. Moreover, the rescue teams always search down the courses of burns first, as that is the most likely place to find a lost person. If you go up and over the shoulder of a hill, you may end up in the back of beyond.

Ski touring and navigation . . .

Cross country skiers and ski mountaineers on the whole read weather conditions more accurately than do downhill skiers and boarders, possibly because they have already assumed responsibility for their own safety. They should be carrying navigation and survival gear, so that if they do get caught by the weather, they have a much better chance of survival if they have to sit it out. Even for the experienced routefinder, navigating on skis is very much more difficult than on foot because seeking out the best snow means you rarely proceed in a straight line, and having to make repeated turns affects your judgement of distance.

If you use a ski centre as a starting point for a ski touring trip, leave a route card with the police or ski patrol, giving your approximate route and the time you expect to return. This is especially important if you plan to stay out overnight, since an unclaimed car at the end of the day could cause a full-scale alert. If you leave your car in a lay-by in a remote spot, you should also leave a route card inside, so that if the police become concerned, they can establish whether or not there is likely to be a problem.

Chapter Six

Rovers, Riders & Racers

Skinny skiers . . .
CROSS COUNTRY SKIERS tend to be a more independent breed than downhillers. So what is the appeal of cross country skiing?

It's probably best understood on the busiest days of winter, when the lift queues stretch endlessly and the nursery slope resembles a vast colony of crippled penguins. It is then that even the most ardent speed freak might begin to look wistfully at the vista of endless shimmering ridges and peaks, and vast untouched snowfields . . . and suddenly the thought of carving your own tracks over all that virgin snow is practically irresistible. Or maybe, after a good snowfall, on a run of brilliant, crisp days, the lure of the quiet forest trails begins to pull you. Or perhaps you're bored with ordinary piste-bashing and you want something a bit more challenging.

. . . days when "the nursery slope resembles a vast colony of crippled penguins . . ."

So how do you go about it if you decide to join the ranks of the eccentric oddballs who walk straight up hills on pathetically undernourished skis and vanish down distant corries performing odd little curtseys?

There are different types of cross country skiing, including off-piste free-heel and telemark, touring, ski mountaineering, trail skiing and racing. Using lighter equipment than downhill, cross country often comes closer to walking or running in its appeal. As in other sports, the standard of equipment has come a long way since the early days, and it is only by talking to experts and trying out different options

---

NORDIC SKI CENTRES IN SCOTLAND

CAIRNWELL (NORDIC) SKI SCHOOL, Gulabin Lodge, Glenshee,
By Blairgowrie, Perthshire PH10 7QE
Tel/Fax 01250 885255/6

GLENMULLIACH NORDIC SKI CENTRE, Stronavaich,
Tomintoul, Banffshire AB37 9ES
Tel/Fax 01807 580356

HUNTLY NORDIC SKI CENTRE, Hill of Haugh, Huntly,
Aberdeenshire AB54 4SH
Tel: 01466 794428; Fax 01466 792180

SCOTTISH NORWEGIAN SKI SCHOOL, Speyside Sports,
64 Grampian Road, Aviemore, Inverness-shire PH22 1PD
Tel: 01479 810656(D)/872309(E); Telex 01479 873415

---

that you'll find what suits you best. There are a number of Nordic ski centres where you can get equipment hire and tuition, or you can buy a ski trail map and go off on your own.

Highland Guides of Inverdruie, Aviemore (on the Coylumbridge road) offer courses, sales and equipment hire. Tel: 01479 810729, Tel/Fax: 811153.

A number of hotels, guest houses and hostels also offer cross country skiing packages. Details of these can be obtained from area tourist information centres (see ski area notes – end sections).

The Alpine option . . .

Ski mountaineering, which demands the most robust equipment of all, brings together the skills of both skier and mountaineer. In its extreme form it can be one of the toughest and most demanding ways of exploring the mountain environment, but even for those whose appetites do not extend to backpacking their skis up sheer ice faces in order to reach the ultimate ski run, there is still plenty of scope to open up new vistas.

Although there is a dedicated band of extremely skilled ski mountaineers who use nordic equipment for even the most extreme situations,

"... the eccentric oddballs who walk straight up hills
on pathetically undernourished skis and vanish
down distant corries performing odd little curtsies ..."

most ski mountaineering in Scotland is done on Alpine equipment. Specialist ski mountaineering skis are benefitting from the same advances in technology as other sports equipment, so technophiles will want to read up on the latest designs and materials. The skis tend to be shorter, broader and lighter than standard downhill skis and utilise bindings with full heel lift and safety features, plus adhesive soles or skins for climbing. The boots are taller, stiffer and lighter and can be adjusted for climbing. Telescopic poles are pleasantly versatile, and ski crampons, ice axes and boot crampons are also part of the essential hardware.

A possible compromise to get you started is to fit a not-too-long pair of downhill skis with a dual-purpose binding which will clip down for descents but can be freed at the heel for climbing. Along with skins and safety straps, this option will not allow you to become a snow tiger overnight but does offer the chance of taking off into the outback when the slopes are crowded. Beware, however, of doing this unprepared. Not all downhill skiers have the navigation skills and mountain experience to survive if the weather changes; if you have any doubts at all about your experience, investigate the range of mountain skills courses on offer at Glenmore Lodge, Aviemore (Tel: 01479 861276).

The Riding Revolution ...

Snowboarding took its time arriving from the States but it's now here to stay. Predicted to outgrow skiing within a few years, it is easier to master than skiing and attracts a very wide following.

All the Scottish ski centres have taken on snowboarding; they provide instruction and board hire and most have constructed snowboard fun parks so that riders can practise skateboard-style tricks. The resort considered to be best for beginners is the Lecht, while Glencoe has the reputation for being the hottest venue for freestylers, mainly because it has many natural jumps and launching pads. Nevis Range is also favoured by advanced riders, especially since the opening up of the spectacular back corries and the centre's efforts at building two fun parks. Glenshee and Cairngorm, which also have special fun parks, are all-round centres.

The predicted frictions between skiers and boarders have not really materialised. Snowboarding is to be included in the 1998 Winter Olympics and British riders are competing successfully at home and abroad in both dry slope and snow competitions. Following the demise of the Scottish Snowboarding Association, the British Snowboarding Association has taken over co-ordinating snowboarding in Scotland; their organiser is Michael Bates. He is also involved with the very active Lothian Snowboard Division, which organises coaching and competitions at Hillend Dry Ski Slope near Edinburgh. To find out more about training, competitions and other snowboarding activities, contact Michael on 0131 445 4046.

Ski Clubs . . .

Regional ski clubs exist throughout Britain and encompass many types of activity. Some are mainly social clubs while others take the practical side of the sport very seriously, running buses to the slopes at

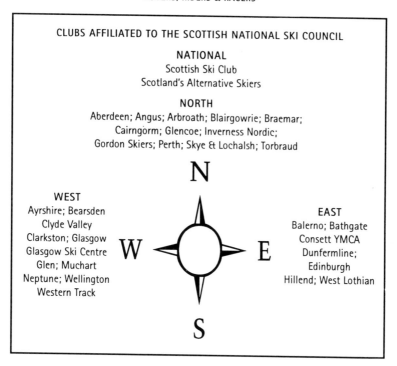

CLUBS AFFILIATED TO THE SCOTTISH NATIONAL SKI COUNCIL

NATIONAL
Scottish Ski Club
Scotland's Alternative Skiers

NORTH
Aberdeen; Angus; Arbroath; Blairgowrie; Braemar;
Cairngorm; Glencoe; Inverness Nordic;
Gordon Skiers; Perth; Skye & Lochalsh; Torbraud

N

WEST
Ayrshire; Bearsden
Clyde Valley
Clarkston; Glasgow
Glasgow Ski Centre
Glen; Muchart
Neptune; Wellington
Western Track

W

E

EAST
Balerno; Bathgate
Consett YMCA
Dunfermline;
Edinburgh
Hillend; West Lothian

S

weekends and involving family members of all ages in recreational and competitive events. Membership of a club is highly recommended to anyone who wants to become more involved in the sport. The clubs in Scotland which are affiliated to the SNSC are listed here by region (see above) – for details of any of them please contact: The Scottish National Ski Council, Caledonia House, South Gyle, Edinburgh EH12 9DQ. Tel: 0131 317 7280; Fax: 0131 339 8602. Their E-mail address is: admin@snsc.demon.co.uk and they have a Web site: http://www.snsc. demon.co.uk.

Further information about Scotland's Alternative Skiers Club can be obtained from: Carol Nickerson, 32 Broomhill Avenue, Aberdeen AB1 6JY. SASC was founded in 1989 to help provide skiing facilities, equipment and opportunities for disabled people in Scotland. Membership is open to anyone from ten years old upwards who has a physical disability, sensory impairment or learning difficulty. Members and helpers train regularly in preparation for a range of winter activities at various Scottish venues, including dry slopes.

Advancing the Art . . .

Skiing, as opposed to snowboarding, usually takes longer to conquer. Perversely perhaps, one of the things many skiers appreciate most about their sport is that, however well you think you ski, there is always more to learn. Those who want to acquire more advanced techniques will find that all the ski schools have highly qualified and experienced instructors available on an hourly basis for individuals and small groups, and it is in this situation that technique improves at an impressive rate.

"It's his pride — as an expert skier he reckons this snowboarding lark should be a doddle — but he's been on that compost heap an awfy long time."

Those who want to go on to become professional ski instructors should contact BASI (the British Association of Ski Instructors) at Glenmore, Aviemore PH22 1QU, Tel. 01479 861717, for full details of their courses and training venues. If you want to become qualified to take groups on snowsporting trips, you should attend a Ski Leader course. Available for Alpine Skiing, Nordic Skiing and Snowboarding, this is a one-week course which offers the best introduction to teaching and leading skiers. For full details contact the Scottish National Ski Council (address at the end of this section).

The Racing Scene . . .

The SNSC is also the co-ordinating body for ski racing, with most races on the Scottish calendar organised by SNSC Clubs and volunteers. Training for racing takes place at all levels of ability and is primarily centred around the ski clubs within Scotland. A number of clubs are affiliated to the SNSC which organises comprehensive training programmes for competitors, the majority of whom are young Alpine racers, though there are enthusiastic and committed groups of Nordic and Freestyle competitors who train in club and squad programmes.

As with all sports development models, there is a pyramid of progression from a wide base of grass roots recreational skiers, up through smaller groups of clubs, to – at the top – the British Ski Team with its handful of dedicated racers.

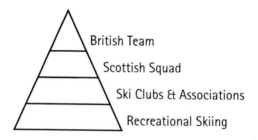

British Team

Scottish Squad

Ski Clubs & Associations

Recreational Skiing

There is a requirement that all ski racers in Scotland must be registered with their national governing body (the SNSC) and have insurance through membership of an affiliated club. Their club training programme should be delivered by a qualified coach, who should hold the SNSC Alpine Performance Coach Level 1 or 2. Clubs which do not have their own APC will either have the services of one or will send their skiers to train with another club. There should be provision for on-slope and artificial slope training on an all-year-round basis, plus physical fitness training when snow training is not possible. Many ski clubs have club buildings on and off the slopes and also offer social events for the parents, recognising their important role in supporting young racers of the future.

A performer can benefit from club training throughout his or her competing career. Even top-class world ski racers like Emma Carrick-Anderson and Andrew Freshwater maintain a close relationship with their home club. However, as not all clubs are equipped to sustain this level of training, at certain levels of performance it may be necessary for a skier to train outside his or her club environment. This is where the SNSC comes in, providing experienced and qualified ski coaches who teach talented racers up to varying levels.

In Scotland, international status has been granted to slopes at Cairngorm, Nevis Range, Glenshee and the Lecht for Slalom and Giant Slalom events.

To get youngsters started, club membership is essential – for details of SNSC-affiliated clubs, contact: The Scottish National Ski Council, Caledonia House, South Gyle, Edinburgh EH12 9DQ. Tel: 0131 317 7280.

Chapter Seven

The Hills are Forever – Or are they?

MOST SKIERS AND SNOWBOARDERS probably never think about what lies under the snow. It is easy to imagine that the hills are just barren, rock-strewn wastes where next-to-nothing grows and that the only wildlife you're likely to come across is a group of Glaswegians having a snowball fight.

Yet the I-Spy spotter's list of species you might hope to find on the hills is surprisingly rich and varied, especially in the Cairngorms. Here the granite plateaus, morainic deposits and glaciated corries have given rise to a very distinctive landscape, supporting an arctic flora and fauna which is unique in Britain and which it shares with very few other places in the world. The inhospitable nature of these mountains has protected them through the ages from exploitation by man and they are now considered to be the most important area for arctic-type wildlife in the EU.

Upland wildlife . . .

What might an ardent amateur naturalist hope to see in the Cairngorms in the course of a year?

At the higher levels, in addition to the expected heaths and lichens, there is a perhaps surprising range of plant, bird and animal species of which the following are examples:

> ptarmigan, mountain hare, dotterel, red deer, snow bunting, meadow pipit, crowberry, wheatear, whortleberry, red grouse, stiff sedge, dunlin, wavy hair grass, golden plover, blaeberry, ring ousel, three-leaved rush, peregrine falcon, dwarf juniper, golden eagle.

Many species of insects, including moths, are found well up the mountainsides, while at lower levels the remnants of the 8,000-year-old Caledonian Pine Forest, with its many lochans, provide habitat for capercaillie, red squirrels, pine martens, wildcats, the Scottish crossbill, crested tits, goldeneye ducks and ospreys. Interesting sightings can easily be had from the ski road between Aviemore and Coire Cas, so if conditions on the hill drive you down from the slopes, even in deepest winter a foray around the shores of Loch Morlich can reveal golden-eye, tufted ducks and whooper swans, plus foraging flocks of smaller birds like bluetits. Listen also for the churring trill of the crested tit. Above the treeline watch out for the Cairngorm herd of reindeer. These were introduced after the second world war as a potential source of meat for the local population and have bred very successfully. So has the pine marten, which in the late 1970s was only found in the far north-west of Scotland. Thanks to the planting of new forests, its numbers have risen dramatically and sightings are now being reported in south Perthshire and beyond.

The pressure points . . .

All these creatures form links in a delicate, complex and inter-twined chain.

> **ANIMALS & BIRDS**
> support
> **AMPHIBIANS, FISH & INSECTS**
> support
> **SOIL, WATER & VEGETATION**

Unfortunately, the parts of this chain most at risk from winter sports are the most fundamental ones – the soil and the vegetation. A fragile carpet of plants is all that stabilises the soil and stops it from being washed away in the extreme mountain weather conditions. Far from protecting the vegetation beneath, as you might imagine it would do, a layer of snow which is subjected to pressure from above and becomes compacted increases soil erosion. Direct damage from skis and snowboards is another problem and is most marked during spring, when the melting snow leaves pieces of vegetation protruding above the surface, ready to be sliced off.

Other problems include disturbance of the soil by skilift installations, access roads and vehicle tracks, and the covering of vegetation with erosion debris. When this happens, a slow recovery can take place over a period of years, provided the depth of the debris is not more than about seven centimetres.

The presence of access roads, chairlifts, car parks, shops and cafés brings increased use of hitherto undisturbed uplands, not just by the downhill snowsports fraternity but also by tourists, hillwalkers and cross-country skiers. This is why conservationists are concerned about the now-discernible outward spread of erosion patterns and the increased encroachment by man into the National Nature Reserves. The spread of litter into these areas has strengthened their argument; old beer cans and polythene bags now congregate around most hilltop cairns, themselves fashioned by rock artists whose skills might have been better employed on garden walls.

Litter around ski areas has been shown to attract scavenging predators such as crows, foxes and gulls, which will move in on an area permanently if there is food to support them. At normal levels, their numbers wouldn't pose a threat to the ground-nesting birds and others of the species noted above, but increased populations do have an effect and concern is being expressed for the welfare of dotterel and ptarmigan chicks in some areas. The chairlift companies go to great lengths and expense to remove all the litter from the hill but the sheer quantity of it is horrifying.

Mountaineering groups and others concerned with the use and management of mountainous areas also resent the impact and intrusion of downhill skiing because it detracts from the wilderness experience, something which is becoming increasingly hard to attain.

The developer's case . . .

The snowsports industry in Scotland continues to be a major growth area in parts of the Highlands where the population was hitherto in decline. Its role in revitalising upland communities, providing jobs and extra trade for a wide range of local businesses, shouldn't be under-estimated. In the Badenoch and Strathspey area alone, it is known that around 180 winter jobs are provided directly by the snowsports industry, which in turn supports, year-round, 2,500 tourism-related jobs. The depopulation in these areas of the Highlands has been reversed, and young people are now able to find jobs near to home instead of having to migrate south.

Anyone who has been on the slopes at peak times will testify that the pressure on the existing facilities is extreme, with queue lengths in some places becoming ridiculous. This gives rise to another point to ponder: if skiers and snowboarders become disenchanted by the length of lift queues, will this prompt more of them to take off into the hinterlands on cross-country skis, or go hill-walking instead? Confining snowsports to a defined area is known to be a favoured method of saving the surrounding areas from harm.

Developers argue that the total area affected by snowsports developments is very small in relation to the vastness of the Scottish Highlands

and that the areas already under conservation designation are suffi-
ciently large to protect the future of the upland environment.

There is no easy solution to the controversy. Campaigns with
emotive titles are snapped up by the media and serve to fuel the popular
image of the conservationists as over-protective, fanatical 'greenies'
and the developers as ruthless, make-a-bomb-out-of-the-tourists
landgrabbers. Both sides have perfectly valid arguments. There is a need
to accommodate more skiing development and it would undoubtedly
benefit the Scottish economy. There is also the ever-present danger
that what man has already done to vast areas of our globe – the Great
Dustbowl, the decimation of the tropical rain forest, the deforested,
eroding Himalayas – will ultimately happen here, in the interests of
commercial gain. And once these areas have been destroyed, they have
gone for ever.

The practicalities . . .

What, then, is being done to try and resolve the conflicts of interest?
Moves have been in play for many years, but not being sensational or
confrontational, they seldom get into the press. In 1984 the Scottish
Development Department published its National Planning Guidelines
on skiing developments in Scotland. Its aim was to reconcile development needs with conservation interests, and the analysis of potential
areas for skiing expansion was based on the Langmuir survey of 1979,
when a group of experts tested out all the areas considered to have
potential and reported on their findings. The then Nature Conservancy
Council provided an inventory of the nature conservation interests in
each area, and the probable impact of skiing development, and Highland Regional Council's Winter Sports Working Party studied skiing
demand and the viability of the various areas.

As a result of all this, guidelines for both primary and secondary
ski areas were drawn up, together with a framework for assessing
development plans and proposals. In 1986 ASH Environmental Design
produced an exceedingly detailed tome entitled 'Environmental Design
and Management of Ski Areas in Scotland – A Practical Handbook' for
the Countryside Commission for Scotland (now Scottish Natural Heritage
– SNH) and Highland Regional Council. Its main function was to provide a planning framework for ski developments and it was compiled
in consultation with a number of bodies, including the Nature Conservancy Council, the chairlift companies, national sports bodies and the
Highlands and Islands Development Board.

The result was a very practical volume, filled with diagrams and a wealth of information on planning and design and on the material and techniques which help to minimise the adverse effects of ski developments on the environment. In 1991 MacKays Agency, Inverness, were commissioned to continue and update this process, taking account of ongoing developments in technology and the results of more recent surveys. Erosion, hydrology, visual impact, wildlife disturbance, pollution and visitor management – all are dealt with in detail, and the handbook is used by the ski centres in their environmental management.

Assessments are made at the beginning and end of every season and the level of awareness of environmental considerations is very high indeed. Summer visitors to ski centres will be able to see the areas which have been re-seeded with native grass seed (which costs over £200 a bag) and the ongoing work which includes litter clearance and footpath maintenance. Heavy equipment is helicoptered into position in order to avoid more ground damage, and snow fencing is chosen to be as unobtrusive as possible, expensive chestnut paling being used rather than cheaper alternatives.

Safeguarding our own future . . .

The destiny of the Scottish hills does not, however, lie purely in the hands of large organisations. The individual snowsports enthusiast, whether downhill skier, snowboarder or cross country skier, can do several things to help safeguard the fragile uplands which support these sports. Maybe you find ludicrous the idea that the odd discarded chocolate wrapper can harm the future of the snowsports industry? Yet consider the fact that 10,000 people may be using a centre in one day; if just one in twenty drops a wrapper, the extent of the litter problem becomes more real. The time spent picking up litter, on the slopes and in the cafés, has to be paid for in the ticket price. In some resorts in the USA users 'buzz' their own tables after meals and are rewarded by cheaper day tickets.

Even bio-degradable litter such as bread crusts, banana skins and apple cores can cause problems because they encourage scavengers like carrion crows and foxes, which in turn inflict casualties on chicks in the spring and summer.

Spring on the hill is a vulnerable time, when patches of bare ground and vegetation begin to show through the snow and the damage done to emerging plants can be very high. It takes the passage of relatively few metal edges to scythe off stems, and once gaps appear, the soil will begin to wash away. It is such a slow, insidious process that as individuals we never notice it, but the cumulative effects of constant passage are considerable. Where a ski area is bounded by a National Nature Reserve or a Site of Special Scientific Interest, it is important to respect the markers and stay within them. A set of tracks setting off into the unknown encourages others to follow. The areas immediately beyond the boundaries would rapidly become degraded were it not for the restrictions, which is why the ski patrols are empowered to confiscate the ticket of anyone found straying.

The wilderness trekker . . .

The cross country skier has an even greater responsibility to the environment, since he or she is venturing into the fragile areas which will show the effects of human impact most rapidly. Not dropping litter and avoiding damage to vegetation are obvious guidelines but less obvious is the need to avoid snow compaction. If a group of skiers is crossing a snow field in single file, each following the track of the leader, there will be a considerably greater impact on the ground than if they spread out. It takes remarkably little time for discernible tracks to appear over such areas, and one single track is more likely to be followed by subsequent skiers.

Another point of which skiers may be less aware is the danger of moving red deer off their wintering grounds. Winter for them means a hard struggle for survival, and the few hours in a day which a herd spends foraging on an area of more productive ground can be vital. Repeated disturbance by skiers or walkers can restrict their grazing range. Grouse and ptarmigan are likewise adversely affected by repeated intrusion into the areas where they congregate in winter.

Taking an interest . . .

An interest in upland wildlife can considerably enhance the snowsporters' enjoyment of a wilderness area and hopefully those who become aware of the potential problems will be willing to make the occasional detour. Who knows, they may even start adding binoculars to their list of essential equipment?

Knowing the issues . . .

The most vital contribution that every individual can make, however, is to become acquainted with the real facts rather than be drawn

'It's not us they should be
putting in cages . . .'

towards any dogma. Sadly, some individuals and organisations have
seized on this debate for their own political ends and the amount of
misinformation in circulation is disturbing. Many of the fiery arguments
which take place in pubs are based on a paucity of knowledge of the
real issues or their background; whereas taking the trouble to find out
could mean replacing a lot of the hot air with the kind of informed
reasoning the whole debate deserves.

We have a unique heritage in our Scottish mountains which we
all want to experience. However, as many populations elsewhere on
this planet have discovered, there is a trick we humans have yet to
master which can be summarised as follows:

"If you want to enjoy it, learn not to destroy it."

PART TWO

The Scottish Skiing
and Snowboarding Centres

GETTING TO KNOW a skiing and snowboarding area takes time – which is what a lot of visitors lack. Most of us can recall the traumas we underwent as beginners, when we tackled a demon draglift for the first time and came a cropper in front of the whole queue, or took a wrong turn onto a blue run and ended up embracing the snowfence. Even experienced skiers and riders can waste time trekking about until they find the pistes that suit them best. To discover that you've just spent ten minutes queuing for a run that takes you three minutes to get down and wasn't very exciting anyway is galling, while nothing is guaranteed to put you off faster than to find yourself with no option but to struggle down near-vertical sheet ice when what you were wanting was a gentle practice area.

When your time available is limited, you want to make the most of it. The following descriptions are intended to give you an insight into each area, and to enable you to make informed choices about where to disport yourself. Have fun!

CAIRNGORM

THE SLOPES AT Cairngorm are just a few miles from Aviemore, reached by a scenic access road which passes through sections of the Old Caledonian pine forest. Since the Cairngorm Chairlift was first opened in December 1961, the expansion of the slopes has led to corresponding developments in accommodation and leisure pursuits in Badenoch and Strathspey, which is now a thriving tourist area.

As you approach the skisport centre, you may like to tune in to Cairngorm Radio Ski FM on 96.6 Kz (local). When you reach the upper section of the access road you'll be faced with the day's first decision: which car park to choose . . . left to Coire na Ciste or right to Coire Cas? At the height of the season you may not have a choice, as the main car park at Coire Cas fills early, but if you are a beginner or intermediate this is the one to aim for anyway, as all the most suitable runs can be reached from here and it is where the ski schools meet, mostly beside the Day Lodge. There is a free bus service between the two car parks and lift tickets can be bought at either.

The main hall of the Day Lodge is where tickets are on sale, and there is also a snack bar, a bar, a restaurant, toilets, ski hire and an equipment shop. The tours of Cairngorm, run by the Cairngorm Ambassador Service, also depart from here. If you are an experienced skier or boarder but have never visited Cairngorm before, the Ambassador Team provide friendly, escorted tours, free of charge. They depart from the Information Office at 10am and 1.30pm daily. At the Day Lodge you can get up-to-the-minute information on the day's conditions and which lifts are likely to be running.

Cairngorm has many facilities for snowboarders, including the Snowboard Bothy which offers hire and instruction. There is a snowboard fun park, usually situated to the right of the Fiacaill T-Bar, but it can be elsewhere, depending on snow conditions. Check with the Bothy instructors or the ski patrol for more information.

Heading up . . .

From the Coire Cas car park there are four routes up the hill. The Car Park Chair is used by beginners and can be very busy even early in the day, and more so at weekends. On all chairlifts children must be accompanied by adults.

CAIRNGORM

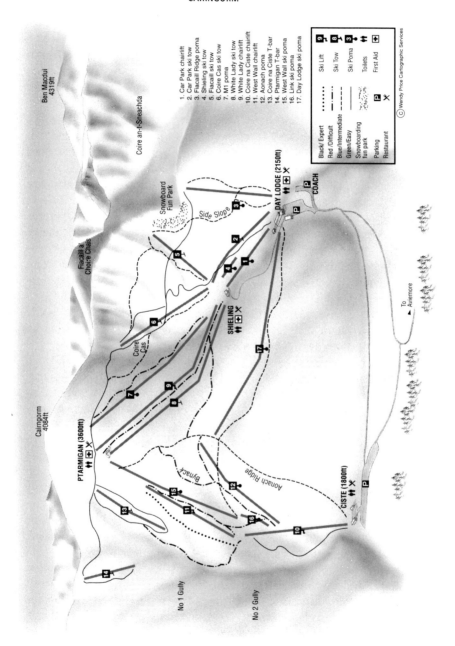

Ben Macdui
4319ft

Coire an-t-Sneachda

1. Car Park chairlift
2. Car Park ski tow
3. Fiacaill Ridge poma
4. Shieling ski tow
5. Fiacaill ski tow
6. Coire Cas ski tow
7. M1 poma
8. White Lady ski tow
9. White Lady chairlift
10. Coire na Ciste chairlift
11. West Wall chairlift
12. Aonach poma
13. Coire na Ciste T-bar
14. Ptarmigan T-bar
15. West Wall ski poma
16. Link ski poma
17. Day Lodge ski poma

Ski Lift
Ski Tow
Ski Poma
Toilets
First Aid

Black/Expert
Red/Difficult
Blue/Intermediate
Green/Easy
Snowboarding
fun park
Parking
Restaurant

© Wendy Price Cartographic Services

Fiacaill a
Choire Chais

Cairngorm
4084ft

Snowboard
Fun Park

Side Slope

Coire
Cas

PTARMIGAN (3600ft)

Bynack

Aonach Ridge

DAY LODGE (2150ft)

COACH

SHIELING

CISTE (1800ft)

To
Aviemore

No 1 Gully

No 2 Gully

If you venture outside the designated ski-patrolled area, this is at your own risk. It is advised that you familiarise yourself with the boundaries before setting out by checking the large piste maps displayed at the centre.

The Fiacaill Ridge Poma is a fast alternative for intermediates upwards and takes you above the Fiacaill T-Bar, Coire Cas T-Bar, the M1 Poma, the White Lady Chair and the White Lady T-Bar, all of which are reached by turning left at the top of the poma lift and schussing across one or more of the runs. Before traversing, do check by looking above you so that you will not spoil someone's descent as you cross.

A more direct and steeper line towards the Day Lodge takes you onto a wide, unmarked slope frequently used for race training and minor races. It occasionally holds good powder and can also be reached by turning right off the top of the Fiacaill T-Bar and starting down the ridge to the top of the Poma. This avoids the less exciting lower slopes and larger queues.

Turning right off the Fiacaill Ridge Poma takes you onto a little-used run of fairly even gradient, leading back to the car park, where the turns to the left are longer than those to the right. The snow is frequently soft and unconsolidated, making it a little more difficult than pisted slopes. It is worth an early morning run before the queues from car park level build up too much.

Alternative access to the hill is by the Car Park Tow. Gentle and slow, it has a short downhill section three quarters of the way up which may throw the unwary when they overtake the T-Bar reel. (Stay calm, and bend the knees!) The tow brings you to an area just below the Coire Cas T-Bar queue which can be a bottleneck as relieved beginners pause to contemplate their next heart-fluttering experience. Exit to the left along the track towards the Chairlift Station and the Shieling.

The run back down leads between the fences of the beginners' area where there can be deep gullies at the narrow points with giggling prostrate bodies which have to be avoided.

Passing the bottom of the Shieling Tow and under the Car Park Chairlift you are on an almost flat track. At the end of this you have a choice: right takes you down the gully of a stream which, when filled with snow, is a gentle series of swinging turns, but when incomplete leaves a steeper left hand bank only. It is not unknown for those with limited control to take an early bath! Left takes you towards the Car Park Tow and another gentle slope; in spring this frequently turns to slush and even running water for ten to fifteen yards, with opportunities for learning to water ski. The Car Park Tow, being popular with beginners, can be busy when classes start, so take care to avoid wiping out someone in the queue.

The Day Lodge Poma, which takes you over the ridge to the Aonach Poma, gives access to the runs described in that section.

If you can avoid having to return to the car park at lunchtime, especially in the height of the season, do so. By staying on the mountain you avoid wasting a lot of time queuing to get back up. There are catering facilities at the middle and top Chairlift stations.

In spring and sometimes at the beginning of the season it is not always possible to ski right back to the Day Lodge, so you will need to use the Chairlift, the downhill entrance being on the opposite side of the building from where you alighted.

Coire Cas is an extremely popular run. It is gentle and forgiving at the top with alternative starts depending on snow conditions. It is normal to get off the tow to the right but sometimes possible to start the descent from the left, though the direct line can be narrow and overtaking difficult. The run narrows and steepens at the last quarter, the well-known Gun Barrel. Everybody has their Gun Barrel story. (A potential disaster area is at the top, where you should watch out for people hurtling in at speed from the right.). It moguls quickly but gets pisted when things get too hectic and the prone body count reaches critical levels. Coire Cas is a good run for the competent skier or rider to warm up on, but is to be avoided if you want a memorable and trouble-free last run – unless you happen to be keen on a slalom with erratically-moving human poles.

With good snow cover, it is possible to turn off to the left halfway down the Gun barrel, across the tow track, and ski a wider unmogulled slope back to the queue. If you wish to avoid the Gun Barrel, follow the signs to the left along a series of zig-zag fences back to the bottom. Taking a right turn shortly after joining the zig-zags leads you onto the chicken-run where there are often jumps built for snowboarders.

The Fiacaill T-Bar is a good run once you've mastered the easy slopes. After a short initial traverse to the left of the top of the tow, there is a fairly wide but even descent to the snow fences leading from the top of the Gun Barrel. If snow permits, a more direct route will take you down, but it is generally easier to follow the fences until you've assessed the conditions and possibilities. The Fiacaill T-Bar is also home to the Snowboarders Fun Park, when it holds sufficient snow. By turning right at the top you should find a variety of jumps and at times a boardercross course.

Off to the right at the top of the Fiacaill is the off-piste area of Coire an t Sneachda, where, when it's quiet, you can get an insight

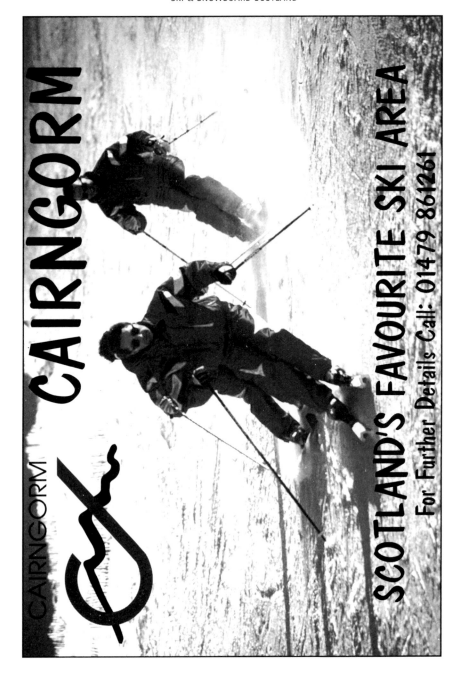

into some of the attractions of cross country skiing. Do remember, however, that this area is not patrolled. You're on your own!

The M1 run was created for racing and is frequently commandeered for this purpose, especially at weekends. It therefore makes little sense to ski it for fun when the flags are out. The M1 Poma gives racers and trainers with priority bibs the right to feed directly into the head of the queue on a one-for-one basis.

The M1 is of a moderate though gradually-increasing gradient on the first half, becoming wider and gentler lower down, before getting steeper again after the timing hut, just above the queue.

Heading further right off the top of this tow takes you along the Traverse, a schuss to the head of Coire Cas. This is the normal descent for relative beginners who have been skiing on the upper slopes of Coire na Ciste. Go into a tuck if there's the slightest headwind as the gradient all but disappears before the sharp bend. Then it's down a short moderate incline onto the narrow road which runs above and parallel to Coire Cas – with a marginally steeper gradient than the piste below.

Left off the M1 Poma takes you onto the White Lady run, a wide moderate slope which moguls with use. At the bottom of this are the Elephant Fences where a high drift offers a relatively safe spot to stop and contemplate the narrower, steeper section which produces the biggest and best moguls. To return to the M1 Tow it is necessary to traverse left well above the bottom of the White Lady; while going straight downhill with a slight relaxation of gradient takes you to the White Lady T-Bar, probably the busiest on the hill.

Having got to the top of the White Lady, there are two ways to approach the White Lady run proper. The direct route along the tow can be relatively snowless at times but saves pushing into a strong westerly wind and tackling the awkward narrows in the snow fences. A longer but more popular track leads more directly away from the right of the lift. It passes under the Chairlift (reserve your slickest party tricks for those watching from above with a critical eye), turns right and narrows into a bottleneck close to where those coming off the M1 also hit the top of the White Lady. This section frequently moguls with no room for error, but just let it flow and you'll find yourself on the upper White Lady.

On rare occasions, snow conditions permitting, it is possible to turn left off the tow, ski the gentle fenced piste to above the Shieling, then drop down a steep, exhilarating slope to just above the Scottish

Ski Club Hut. There are a number of edge-blunting stones on this route and unfortunately this run rarely lasts.

The Ptarmigan and Coire na Ciste area . . .

The area served by the Ptarmigan Tow and the Coire na Ciste Tow consists of a large, gentle bowl which lasts right through to the end of the season. It is not unknown to get reasonable powder in this area and to be able to leave clearly identifiable tracks.

By continuing further along the ridge, expert skiers and riders can find exciting, steep, off-piste challenges in Coire Laogh Mor. These slopes are not included in the patrolled area, so be warned: you venture here at your own risk. The steepest bit (watch you don't bowl over the odd apprentice snow-and-ice climber cutting his way up with ice axes – it has happened!) is found by skating and pushing to the right across the very gentle ridge until you reach the Head Wall. The views to east and west from here are definitely worth a pause. Know the conditions: this wall avalanches, as does the Head Wall of Coire Cas.

A less steep but nonetheless enjoyable descent is gained by dropping off the wide and moderate slope of the East Wall until you find the snow fence leading to your right. Before setting out, make sure the run from Coire Laogh Mor to the Coire na Ciste car park is complete. This run is sometimes posted closed and should not be attempted if the mist has closed in and you are unfamiliar with the geography of the area.

The remaining steep lower half of the East Wall takes you to the bottom of the gully, opposite the board walk from the West Wall Chair. These boards are needed in late spring for access from the end of the Gully (which by then is well mogulled) to the lift, but at the height of the season it is skiable.

The Gully itself is moderately steep but narrow and can catch out intermediates who have found Coire na Ciste easy and the continuation inviting. After it has been filled in by a strong wind, however, it provides a smooth, fast run with escape routes, should these be necessary, up the side walls. This is considered to be the best and quietest area for good skiers and accomplished boarders.

Alternative uplift can be had from this point by using the West Wall Poma which terminates beside the top of the White Lady Tow and therefore aids rapid return to the Cas side of the hill.

If you wish to ski the West Wall only, or the steeper section of the

Gully, the West Wall Chair provides access. The West Wall itself is a broad, steep convex slope which is for better performers only. It can be closed due to ice and notices should be heeded, since a fall under these conditions can be fatal. If you are enjoying a direct and ever-steepening descent, watch out for the stepped 'roads' created by those traversing from the Gully to the West Wall Poma – they can be a severe test on the shock absorbers.

Access to the Wall can be difficult. Turning right off the Chair leads to a snow fence and a short, narrow and frequently rocky descent. Coming left off the Chair usually provides access without dropping all the way into the Gully before finding a traverse to the left. Between the Chair and the Poma the fenced run produces good moguls on a fairly uniform and less steep slope than the Wall itself. The contrast with the other relatively unmogulled side of the Chair is frequently visible from Glenmore.

Aonach, with its Poma, can be reached by the access tow from above the Day Lodge and also by a long and in places very gentle descent from the top of Coire na Ciste, via Windy Ridge, where the White Lady Tow meets the West Wall Poma. Unfortunately, from this vantage point the size of the queue for the Aonach is an unknown quantity, and once down you are committed to wait, unless conditions allow a return to the Ciste car park and a trip back up the Chair, from which the Aonach queue can be seen.

Aonach is a broad bowl with a steep start and a concave fall line. Skiers normally get off to the left of the tow, begin with a traverse, and break off when they find a free line. When snow is scarce, the gentle lower slope narrows, but beware the final short descent into the queue, particularly when the tops of the snow fence are sticking through. This tow line is the lowest on the hill, so is usually the last to be complete and the first to break.

From the top of the Aonach, access to the Shieling area can be gained by following the signs and snow fences to the right. A challenging steep slope to the left can provide an interesting descent in the right conditions. From the bottom of Aonach or the Gully it is also possible, on a gentle but tricky schuss, to reach the restaurant at Coire na Ciste car park.

The Coire na Ciste Chair is not for the inexperienced. The ascent is made with skis on, and to alight you slide down a ramp. Downhill passengers are taken on the lower Chair but there is no such facility on the upper, except in an emergency. Beginners using this route for access to the gentle upper slopes frequently have difficulty returning to the car park. It is not uncommon to see a pathetic figure, hugging skis, plodding laboriously down beside the West Wall. If there is any ice around, this is a dangerous method of descent, so instead, head for the Traverse, then down Coire Cas and the Car Park Run to the Day Lodge, from which there is a free bus service back to Coire na Ciste car park.

The facilities for eating on the hill are good considering the numbers catered for. The Day Lodge, Shieling, Ptarmigan and Coire na Ciste have cafés and there is room for eating packed lunches under cover. The Scottish Ski Club has a hut just above the Shieling which provides shelter and catering for members and their guests.

Enquiries about skiing at Cairngorm to:

INFORMATION, CAIRNGORM CHAIRLIFT COMPANY,
Aviemore, Inverness-shire PH22 1RB
Tel. 01479 861261
Ski Hotline: 0891 654 655 (*Calls cost 50p per minute*)
Fax Back: 0897 500614 (*Calls cost £1 per minute*)
Cairngorm Radio Ski FM 96.6 (*local*)
Ceefax Page 431
Web sites: www.aviemore.co.uk
www.holiday.scotland.net/activities/ski

AVIEMORE TOURIST INFORMATION CENTRE
Grampian Road, Aviemore PH22 1PP
Tel: 01479 810363 (*24 hrs*)
Fax: 01479 811063
Nearest 24-hour petrol station: Aviemore.

GLENCOE

FOR VARIED AND CHALLENGING snowsports in a compact area, Glencoe has a lot to offer. It has a long skiing history: in the 1930's the Creag Dubh Mountaineering Club and the Lomonds Club used Ba Cottage as a doss and the base for their skiing activities, amid good-natured rivalry. These two clubs eventually gave birth to the Glencoe Ski Club and the White Corries Rescue Patrol, and before long the Scottish Ski Club joined in the action. Frith Finlayson set up his ski school and Glencoe became the focus for Glasgow-based skiers. Today it still draws many of its devotees from the banks of the Clyde, but its enormously-improved uplift facilities and runs, together with the fact that, thanks to the Plateau Poma, you no longer have to walk across the Plateau, mean that it caters for a much wider public. Glencoe also has two pisting machines, which have made a significant difference to its snow preparation and holding capabilities.

Glencoe is open seven days a week, 8.30am to 5pm. At car park level you will find the ski school, restaurant, hire shop and ticket office; the latter also sells items such as gloves, hats, goggles, socks and suncream – i.e. all those small but important items that people tend to forget. There is disabled access and a telephone, and the centre offers package deals on hire, instruction and uplift with major discounts.

The slopes are reached by a modern double-seater chairlift installed in 1991. It has an uplift capacity of 1,186 passengers per hour and will deposit you near the Plateau Poma and the Beginner's Tow. If you want to go straight to the main runs, the Plateau Tow will take you there, but if you're relatively new to skiing and snowboarding you may want to stay on the two lower runs to build up your confidence on their gentle, well-pisted slopes.

For snowboarding, Glencoe has such superb natural freestyle terrain that there has been no need to construct special snow parks – it's all there ready-made! Beginners will soon gain confidence on the Plateau runs and then it's on to Mug's Alley for the next stage. Good freestyle areas are The Canyon, which includes the 'bum-hole', The Wall and Thrombosis. Glencoe is also very popular for freeriding on account of the concentrated access leading to such a wide variety of open terrain. The steep, fast gully of The Canyon is again recommended, together with the Main Basin, Happy Valley, Rannoch Glades, Etive Glades and

GLENCOE

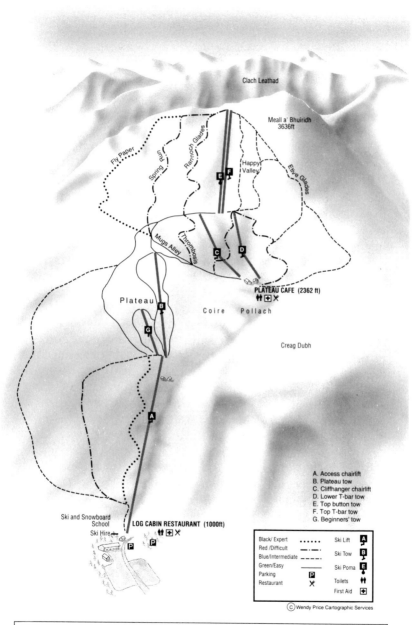

Clach Leathad

Meall a' Bhuiridh
3636ft

Fly Paper

Spring Run

Rannoch Glades

Happy Valley

Etive Glades

E F

Mugs Alley

Thrombosis

C D

PLATEAU CAFE (2362 ft)

Plateau

B

G

Coire Pollach

Creag Dubh

A

Ski and Snowboard School
Ski Hire

LOG CABIN RESTAURANT (1000ft)

P P

A. Access chairlift
B. Plateau tow
C. Cliffhanger chairlift
D. Lower T-bar tow
E. Top button tow
F. Top T-bar tow
G. Beginners' tow

Black/ Expert	....	Ski Lift	A
Red /Difficult	_._._.	Ski Tow	B
Blue/Intermediate	_ _ _		
Green/Easy	_____	Ski Poma	E
Parking	P		
Restaurant	X	Toilets	
		First Aid	

© Wendy Price Cartographic Services

If you venture outside the designated ski-patrolled area, this is at your own risk. It is advised that you familiarise yourself with the boundaries before setting out by checking the large piste maps displayed at the centre.

the red Access Chair run. Subsequently, good alpine riding can be had on runs such as Etive Glades, Happy Valley and the Main Basin.

For the extreme experience, Fly Paper (Scotland's steepest on-piste run) and the black Access Chair run both offer exciting but accessible challenges for the skilled and courageous.

Developments . . .

The Plateau is the hub of the centre and the focal point for some exciting development plans for more tows, a chairlift across the Plateau and a 250-seater restaurant. The existing 'Cliffy' Chairlift is also to be upgraded in terms of capacity and diverted to provide easier access to the Top T-Bar and the Button Tow. The Top Button Tow is to be replaced with a high-speed tow, and a new tow on Etive Glades is planned to give exclusive access to what is an excellent blue run. Access to this tow would be either from the existing upper tows or a link tow in front of Creag Dubh, with a trainer tow which would originate from below the existing Lower Tow.

From the top of the Plateau Tow you can ski to the Cliffy Chairlift which is the gateway to many of Glencoe's varied runs.

Mug's Alley

Starting with the easy runs, Mug's Alley provides a nice warm-up for the first few runs of the day and, as its name implies, is very popular with less confident skiers and riders. Mug's Alley is often the first run higher up the hill for those progressing from the easy slopes of the Plateau. The gradient on one side is steeper than on the other, giving a choice of descents, and the run culminates in the Canyon under the Cliffy Chairlift. You can distinguish the Canyon by the number of 'big air' enthusiasts.

Etive Glades

Etive Glades is a very worthwhile run, long and scenic, taking you further out than the other runs and swinging down between rocky ridges. To reach it, turn right off the Top T-Bar, stay high, and then ski down as far to the left as possible.

Happy Valley

When the snow is good, Happy Valley is a great run. Regular pisting makes it a joy to ski and there is endless scope for both skiers and snowboarders to play here. The run fans out into a number of descents,

Ski & Board Scotland's Original, Est. 1959
glencoe
▲ BIG VALUE mid-week packages.
▲ Wide Range of Accommodation.
▲ "The Fly Paper is arguably the best run in Scotland, while the Haggis Trap is always fun."
The Good Ski Guide A–Z, 1997.
▲ Open 7 Days.
For Further Information Contact:
Glencoe Ski Centre
Kinghouse, Glencoe, Argyll, Scotland, PA39 4HZ
Enquiries: 01855 851 226. Fax: 01855 851 233
Ski Hotline: 0891 654 658. Ski Report: 01855 851 232
SKI SCOTLAND
Ski Lochaber
glencoe

so you can choose your own way down. At the bottom of Happy Valley is 'The Narrows': as the name suggests, the width of the piste decreases into a winding defile. Before the arrival of the pisting machine, this used to be the site of the monster moguls that were capable of swallowing skiers.

Main Basin

This runs directly down the side of the top tows and offers a wide area for cruising, with some interesting terrain mixed in – ideal for bumps and jumps! It leads you to the Haggis Trap, though the less brave can escape by traversing to Happy Valley. Usually the first indication of the Haggis Trap is the sudden appearance of a body launching out of a hole in the ground. Viewed from downhill, you get the full effect of gritted teeth, contorted expressions and, quite often, crash landings. The Haggis Trap is best described as a small gully with vertical entry and exit, where you're guaranteed to part company with your stomach.

Rannoch Glades

This is a gentle run between the Main Basin and the Spring Run. It's interesting to pick your way between the rocks in search of untouched snow, of which there's usually plenty. You can either cut off to the left near the bottom to rejoin the upper tows or carry on down a steeper section to rejoin Mug's Alley.

The Spring Run

To find the Spring Run you turn left off the top of the Top T-Bar and traverse east across the hill, on a track which leads through the stones. The Spring Run is somewhat steeper than Happy Valley with fewer moguls and is especially good for those sticky, porridgey days, because the extra steepness provides more momentum. As its name suggests, in spring snow this is a superb run. You have the option near the bottom of going back to the Top T-Bar or heading on down Mug's Alley.

Flypaper

No prizes for guessing that this is the steepest on-piste run in Scotland. It is short but quite vicious, with rocks poking out halfway down. Fall here in icy conditions and you'll be more than lucky to escape unscathed. Waist deep in powder, however, it's a dream run and, like the Canyon and the Haggis Trap, is popular with the lunatic schoolies.

Another reasonably demanding run, as yet un-named, is to the left of the Cliffy Chair; it's well worth it just to ski moguls through soft powder snow, clinging to an almost vertical slope. One of the great things about Glencoe is that you can literally make up runs as you go along and there's plenty of variety, from the very long east-side runs to the headbangers' specials.

A 100-seater licensed log cabin restaurant near the foot of the Access Chairlift serves hot meals, snacks and drinks, including gluhwein, all day. The Plateau Café also serves hot and cold snacks, and there are toilets there as well. The Scottish Ski Club has a hut close to the top of the Cliffy which provides catering for members only.

For enquiries about skiing and snowboarding, contact:

GLENCOE SKI CENTRE,
Kingshouse, Glencoe, Argyllshire PA39 4HZ
Tel: 01855 851226
Fax: 01855 851 233
Ski Centre Weather and Snow report: 01855 851 232
Ski Hotline 0891 654 658 (*calls cost 50p per minute*)
Metcall Ski Scotland: 0336 411200
Web site: www.ski.scotland.net

GLENSHEE

THE FULL EXTENT of the Glenshee snowfields is not immediately apparent on arrival. Having travelled through the splendours of Royal Deeside, or negotiated the winding A93 from the south, the final climb to the car parks brings you to a height of 2,199 feet, making it the highest point in Britain to be reached by a main road. The uplift system extends not only over the slopes visible from the car park but into two further glens over the back of Sunnyside, opening up a wide variety of excellent runs and snowfields for all grades of skiers and snowboarders.

Skiing first began in the Glenshee area in the late 1930s, when a few enthusiasts who had learned to ski in Europe came to practise their skills in their native Scotland. It is said that the first tow to be installed at Glenshee was on Mount Blair and it was also the first of many home-made tows driven off the rear wheels of motor cycles or tractors anchored at the top of the slope. Various ski clubs (Perth, Dundee and Aberdeen) constructed such tows in the snow-holding gullies during the post-war era; they were the type which often indiscriminately shredded gloves and fingers and were greatly frowned upon by the purists who considered that using mechanical uplift was cheating. Nevertheless, in spite of its propensity for lengthening arms, the tow became popular and was the start of an expansion in the late 1950s, when Dundee Ski Club erected the first T-Bar on Meall Odhar. In 1961 several of the current directors, in conjunction with Invercauld Estate, formed the Glenshee Chairlift Company, and the Cairnwell Chairlift and a small café were built. In the winter of 1962 the Company opened these to the public and Glenshee's rise towards ultimately running Britain's largest network of lifts and tows had begun.

Glenshee now has uplift capacity for over 18,500 persons per hour, covers an area of 790 hectares, and has seven snowmaking cannons which can cover 20,000 square metres of the hillside, offering snow for 200-500 skiers. A computerised ticket system and an additional ticket desk in the hire shop have been installed to reduce queuing time. At the base level, by the car parks, there is the licensed Glenshee Base Café, ticket office, ski and snowboard rental, ski and snowboard school, equipment shop, first aid post, ski patrol, crèche and telephone. On the Cairnwell side is the Cairnwell Mountain Restaurant,

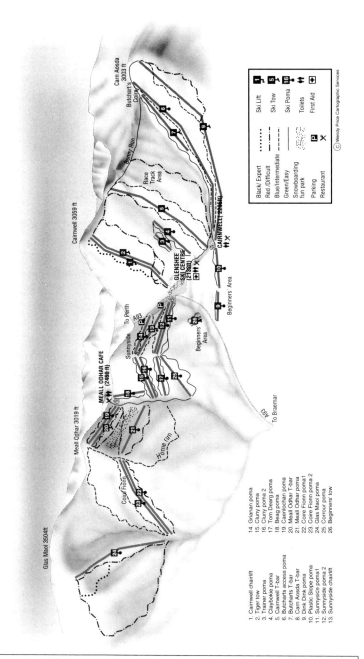

Legend:

Ski Lift	
Ski Tow	
Ski Poma	
Toilets	
First Aid	

Black/Expert ....
Red/Difficult – · – · –
Blue/Intermediate – – –
Green/Easy
Snowboarding fun park
Parking
Restaurant

© Wendy Price Cartographic Services

Map labels:

Carn Aosda 3003 ft
Butchart's Coire
Tinny Run
Race Track Area
Cairnwell 3059 ft
CAIRNWELL (2965ft)
GLENSHEE SKI CENTRE (2139ft)
Beginners' Area
To Perth
Sunnyside
Beginners' Area
MEALL ODHAR CAFE
MEALL ODHAR (2460 ft)
Meall Odhar 3019 ft
Home run
Coire Fionn
Glas Maol 3504ft
To Braemar
A93

1. Cairnwell chairlift
2. Tiger tow
3. Trainer poma
4. Claybokie poma
5. Cairnwell T-bar
6. Butchants access poma
7. Butcharts T-bar
8. Carn Aosda T-bar
9. Dink Dink poma
10. Plastic Slope poma
11. Sunnyside poma 1
12. Sunnyside poma 2
13. Sunnyside chairlift
14. Grianan poma
15. Cluny poma
16. Cluny poma 2
17. Tom Dearg poma
18. Beag poma
19. Caenlochan poma
20. Meall Odhar T-bar
21. Meall Odhar poma
22. Coire Fionn poma 1
23. Coire Fionn poma 2
24. Glas Maol poma
25. Cornour poma
26. Beginners' tow

If you venture outside the designated ski-patrolled area, this is at your own risk. It is advised that you familiarise yourself with the boundaries before setting out by checking the large piste maps displayed at the centre.

which is licensed and has toilet facilities, while over at Meall Odhar is the Meall Odhar Mountain Café, again with toilet facilities.

A nice touch is the Food Events which occur at the restaurants and cafés approximately every two weeks, when foreign and speciality themes are on offer. Mexican Magic takes place fortnightly on Wednesdays at Meall Odhar Mountain Café while Pizza & Pasta is weekly on Fridays at Cairnwell Mountain Restaurant. The latter is also the venue for 'Rugby Live', when compulsive rugby fans can watch the game live on TV without missing their day on the snow. Other events are on offer throughout the season – full details are available from the centre.

With its huge snow area and variety of terrain, Glenshee is now an extremely popular resort for snowboarders of all standards. Beginners have a wide range of tows and runs to choose from (see details below); for freestylers there are natural quarter pipes on Butcharts and the Plastic Slope, and runs such as Coire Fionn and Glas Maol provide long, fast freeriding areas. For 'steep' fanatics, the black runs on the Tiger, Glas Maol and Carn Aosda give some of the steepest runs in Scotland. Established in 1991, the Snowboard Fun Park at Meall Odhar is set to ride like a boardercross when conditions permit, featuring gap jumps, banked turns, a quarter pipe and much more.

In spite of its size and popularity, Glenshee is a friendly resort. The runs are well-tended by an armada of snow-grooming machines and the wide-open spaces give a pleasantly uncluttered feeling, even when the tows are operating to capacity.

The first question of the day at Glenshee is which side of the road to ski. Both sides offer a full spectrum for all abilities, but since the opening up of the Glas Maol area there has been a tendency for the crowds to make a beeline for the Sunnyside Chairlift and Pomas in the morning, leaving the Cairnwell relatively queue-free. Your choice of destination will depend largely on your skill level

For complete beginners, the best course is to book lessons at one of the ski schools (see relevant section). If there's time to kill before your lesson, the nursery slopes adjoining the car park or on the Braemar side of the café are as good as any. Check that the run-out doesn't end in the burn or on the road. Once you've found your feet and want to try a little uplift, the Dink Dink Poma, Claybokie, the Beginner's Tow and the Trainer Tow on Cairnwell are ideal. The Glenshee Ski and Snowboard School has priority on the former, so at busy times it is worth taking the Plastic Slope Poma up to Claybokie and the Trainer Tow.

At the top of the Plastic Slope Poma, looking towards the slopes you will find the Carn Aosda T-Bar up on your right. In anti-clockwise direction from here you'll find: Butchart's Access Poma, Butchart's T-Bar (higher up and out of sight from here), Cairnwell T-Bar, Claybokie Poma, the Trainer Poma, the Tiger Tow and, way over to the left, the Cairnwell Chairlift.

For improvers, or for a pleasant warm-up, The Butchart's Access Poma is excellent, offering a number of possible descents depending on snow cover. Leaving the tow to the left you can ski down beside it, pick yourself a route further out, or follow the top snow fence along to the top of the Butchart's T-Bar run. Here there are two alternatives. For those who wish to avoid the short steep section at the top, it is possible to descend into a little bowl beside the upper tow and then cross the tow line – carefully, as there is often a lip here from which snowboarders launch themselves.

Although short, Butchart's holds its snow well and the steep bit to the left of the top of the tow is popular with budding short-swingers and confidence-gaining boarders. The run itself splits into two lower down and joins up again by the tow hut. Here you have the choice of either going back up the T-Bar or returning down the flank of the gully to the Access Poma.

Carn Aosda, another T-Bar tow, offers a demanding run because of its steep upper section. The main run can be reached by turning left off the tow and side-stepping up to a broad, well-marked track which curves around the summit of the hill. Just before it meets the snow-fence you can break off to the left on a steepish traverse which will bring you to the fenced runs parallel to the tow. If the upper traverse doesn't take your fancy, you have the option of carrying on beside the snowfence to Butchart's.

The more adventurous (and hopefully skilled) can leave the Carn Aosda T-Bar to the right and descend a shallow gully before choosing whether to head straight down, crossing the tow at a lower point, or cross it higher up and brave the steep bit above the run. Watch out for rocks here when the snow cover is thin.

When snow cover is good, it is also possible for the expert to stay high and explore descents a little further out, but be aware that this takes you off-piste and therefore outside the ski-patrolled area, leaving you responsible for your own welfare. Sometimes early-morning powder can be found here; witness the graceful S-trails left by devotees of the steeps.

SCOTLAND'S LARGEST LIFT SYSTEM

Ski & Snowboard Glenshee

Glenshee is Scotland's most extensive
ski area with 38 pistes across
3 valleys with a wide variety of runs
from gentle beginners slopes
to exciting and challenging runs
for experienced skiers and boarders.

- 40km downhill runs
- 26 lifts
- 7 artificial snow making cannons
- 5 Kassbohrer piste grooming machines
- Free parking for 1400 cars and 50 coaches
- Equipment hire and tuition

Glenshee Ski Centre Cairnwell, Braemar,
Aberdeenshire AB35 5XU

Enquiries: **013397 41320** (5 lines)
Ski Report: 013397 41628
Fax: 013397 41665

For more information on skiing
in Grampian Highlands
and to book accommodation
Tel: 0990 39 33 39

For the latest SNOW CONDITIONS Report,
visit our Web site – www.ski.scotland.net

glensh'ee
SKI CENTRE

SKI SCOTLAND
Grampian Highlands

SCOTLAND'S
three VALLEYS

86

The Cairnwell T-Bar provides access to the northern end of the Cairnwell ridge, giving a number of possible descents. The first of these is the run to the left of the tow, steep and heavily-mogulled at the top and running out to a longish level piste which is often very ego-flattering. Those who chicken out of the moguls can cruise along the ridge and pick a more discreet place to turn and head back to the run, or descend to Claybokie or the Trainer Tow.

On the right of the tow there is a blue run, quite narrow between the snowfences, where the race courses are laid out. Most of the time there is access to these but when there's a race on, you are asked to keep off. The public race course, which begins at a little A-framed hut, is operated by tokens which are bought from Glenshee Ski Centre Ski and Snowboard School and can be used any time there are not races in progress. The automatic timing device gives you a readout of your time when you reach the bottom.

Cairnwell is often used for racing, particularly at weekends, and racers have priority on the tow, so at such times it's advisable to move on to one of the other lifts.

A pleasant and easier route from the top of Cairnwell involves schussing down the side of the snowfence and staying up on the ridge until the next fenced slope is reached. This often holds good snow and comes out slightly higher up the gully than the Butchart's Access Poma. If, however, you continue along the ridge, you will find a pleasant trail with an outback feel to it as it leads you up one side of the gully and back down the other to Butchart's T-Bar. Braver souls can peel off and seek a jump or two in the gully.

The run for which Glenshee is perhaps most famous is the Tiger, and it is reached by either the Cairnwell Chairlift or the Tiger Tow. The single-seater Chairlift is for adults and over-eight-year-olds only. Remember that the temperature at the top station may be a good bit lower than at the car park, so dress accordingly. You can check the summit wind speed on a dial in the bottom station window. When the ice warning sign is out it should be heeded, especially by anyone who admits to being something less than an expert.

Since the installation of the Tiger Button Tow, which starts further up the hill above the Chairlift station, pressure on the Chairlift has reduced and the queues tend not to get so long. Nevertheless, anyone coming down the gully from the direction of Claybokie should slow down before whistling round the last bend in order to avoid colliding with people queuing. If you don't feel like walking up to the Tiger Tow, you can reach it either by going up the Plastic Slope and Cairnwell T-Bar and skiing down, or by taking the Chairlift.

Whichever uplift you use, you have three choices at the top of the Tiger: to head off to the right along the ridge back to the Cairnwell T-Bar run, to descend the right hand side of the Tiger Tow, or to tackle the Tiger itself.

The traverse to Cairnwell can be reached by either of the two tracks to the right, and once on the traverse it's a case of heading for where the snow seems best. When there's plenty of snow, it is possible to pick out a number of routes, but the most reliable one lies closest to the tow. Steep and narrow, it can be a taxing run and is definitely for the proficient.

The Tiger itself is one of the best runs in Scotland, and when it's in good condition, it really cannot be beaten for sheer exhilarating enjoyment. There are, of course, days when sheet ice, windslab and frozen rutted moguls make it less than a doddle but you will still see people skiing it – and often well! The Tiger is a run that epitomises the ultimate challenge of Scottish snowsports, i.e., being able to handle a whole range of different conditions competently.

To get to the Tiger, you duck under the Chairlift and immediately are on a broad and not-too-fierce slope where you can sort out the rhythm before the fun starts. After you've knocked the (hopefully) big moguls into shape, or collected yourself after they've done that to you, head for the narrower fenced run where the bumps tend to be smaller, and so down to the Chairlift again – or across to the Tiger Tow. An alternative to the upper mogulfield is to head towards the snow fence and ski the flatter snow further across, cutting back in time to regain the lower run. In certain snow conditions this route is superb.

Sunnyside and beyond . . .

The eastern side of the road has developed beyond recognition since the early 1970s. The always-popular Sunnyside is reached by a double poma, for which the queues are long at busy times. From the top, there are five possible take-off points. Turning left from the tow, you can ski the run nearest to it or take the slightly more level route northwards along the top of the hill and follow the next fenced run down. Both of these routes meet at what can be a bottleneck, so control and caution are necessary to avoid accidents. The rest of the run from here is easy going.

Going straight ahead at the top of Sunnyside takes you to the tops of two runs which go over the back of the hill. These are Corrour and Tom Dearg, both served by pomas and excellent for beginners wanting to gain confidence. Tom Dearg at times has quite a long queue when those who have been further over at Coire Fionn choose to return to the car park via the home run, which arrives at the foot of Tom Dearg Poma.

Also from the top of Sunnyside Poma, it is possible to ski to the right, at the back of the hill, along a very gently fenced slope which leads to the Cluny run, popular with improving beginners and intermediates. The final option off Sunnyside is to descend the right hand slope, an excellent route back down to the Chairlift. The wooden building near the foot of this slope is the Scottish Ski Club Hut, open to members only.

The Sunnyside Chairlift is a double chair, on which children have to be accompanied by an adult. For very small or nervous people the lift attendant will normally slow the chair down to enable them to get on without trauma.

At the top, if you want to go back down to the car park, you have two options, basically left or right, and both intermediate runs. The furthest to the right can take you down to the Grianan Poma, a very under-used tow giving access to an excellent run which remains relatively undiscovered. It is worth looking to see how busy it is when there are queues elsewhere.

Over the back of Sunnyside Chair lie the green runs which descend on both sides of the Cluny Pomas. To the left, along the top of the hill, are routes leading to the Corrour and Tom Dearg runs, described earlier, while Cluny is a great favourite with skiers at the snowplough stage and newly-fledged riders. If, however, you have small children who are just beginning to get to grips with skiing, the gentle Beag Poma, which links the bottom of Cluny with the Meall Odhar Café, is ideal.

Near the start of the Beag Poma, up a bank, is Meall Odhar Poma. This is the main route for getting over the back to Coire Fionn and Glas Maol. (An alternative route at busy times is up the Beag and then the Caenlochan Poma or its adjacent Meall Odhar T-Bar.) The full potential of the Meall Odhar Poma runs is largely untapped, which is a pity since there are some excellent red runs, especially on the north side of the tow.

To begin with the most obvious, however, you can leave the tow on either side. A steepish descent into mogulfields follows, sometimes cut up by transverse ridges made by people coming across the hill at a more gentle angle. In good snow a number of excellent variations are possible when descending to the left of the tow on the northern side. Or, when ready to head back to the car park, you can take the signposted Meall Odhar Return route or "Back Passage" as it is affectionately known by the staff. This is a long, well-pisted route which sweeps round the side of the hill and ends up at the Tom Dearg Poma.

Heading southwards, by picking a higher route round the shoulder of the hill, you can take one of a number of traverses over to Meall Odhar, where there are toilets and a café. From here, the Meall Odhar T-Bar and Caenlochan Poma provide access to their own red runs, to the Snowboard Fun Park and to the whole Glas Maol area over the back.

'Over the back', as most people refer to it, is a wide basin of snow where a whole spectrum of runs await you.

Facing the top of the double Coire Fionn Poma, from Meall Odhar Poma, the route nearest the tow is the main run. Deceptively smooth and easy at the top, it gets more interesting over the brow, where moguls often build up between the snowfences. The other side of the poma provides a descent of similar gradient, with a few variations possible depending on snowcover. The gentlest run is reached by a long traverse to the head of the corrie. As you lose height you will notice a deep gully below you, known as the Gun-Barrel, where figures can be seen zig-zagging from side to side (and occasionally popping out over the rim with a screech), a tactic which soon becomes addictive. You need to keep your wits about you here as you don't want your zig to coincide with someone else's zag.

The Glas Maol Poma gives access to some excellent runs for intermediates and above. The lift reaches right to the boundaries of the National Nature Reserve, hence the markers beyond which skiers and snowboarders are banned. Ignoring these can lead to the confiscation of your ticket.

At the top of the poma the only way off is to the left, where there is ample space to adjust the lug-warmers and admire the view before taking any decision about where to go. Immediately to the left is a gap in the snowfence. This leads onto the shoulder above the first (black) run and gives a fast descent which usually has good snow cover.

The wide schuss from the top of the tow leads to all the other routes. First left is the black run, marked 'Experts Only'. Narrow at first, it quickly gives way to a wide, usually mogulled basin with opportunities for some good descents off the side walls. Further down you can choose between the gully and the slope above it, where powder sometimes lurks.

A second demanding descent is reached just beyond the mid-section of the ridgetop schuss and is marked by a suitable gap in the snowfence. This is a steep descent off the shoulder and is often at its best early in the day, when you have the chance to make your own snake-trail. It provides some excellent skiing, but being less well used it is sometimes be subject to crusting and may require crud skills and stamina.

The main red run, at the end of the schuss, is good for warming up early in the day and tends to soften earlier because of its popularity. On the schuss, since there is a slight incline at the far end, you'll need to get into a tuck to keep up your impetus if there's any head wind at all. Watch out for people taking a sharp left onto the above runs. The red run begins at the top of a wide horseshoe which can be descended from any point along the ridge. Good snow conditions make this an immensely popular playground and it can absorb a surprisingly large number of skiers without appearing congested. In icy conditions the line down the gully is usually the first to soften up, although the untouched snow further along the ridge, while steep, usually provides a grip. At the foot of the gully is a minor gun barrel which can provide jumps.

For further information about skiing and snowboarding, contact:

GLENSHEE SKI CENTRE,
Cairnwell, Braemar, Aberdeenshire AB35 5XU
Tel: 013397 41320
Fax: 103397 41665
Web site: www.ski.scotland.net
Snow, Road and Weather Conditions
Metcall Ski Scotland: 0336 411200
Glenshee Ski Centre Report: 013397 41628
Ski Hotline: 0891 654 656 (*calls cost 50p per minute*)

Accommodation Enquiries
Aberdeen & Grampian Tourist Board: 01330 825917
Perthshire Tourist Board: 01738 444144

General Tourist Enquiries
Braemar Tourist Information: 013397 41600
Blairgowrie Tourist Information: 01250 875800;
Fax: 01250 873701

Joint Glenshee and Glencoe season tickets are available, plus other joint offers and discount packages with many different combinations of lift tickets, hire and instruction at competitive prices.

Nearest petrol and diesel: The Spittal Hotel and Braemar Service Station (the latter has a 24hr breakdown service, Tel: 013397 41210). Fuel is also available in Blairgowrie. The nearest 24-hour fuel station is in Perth.

THE LECHT

THE LECHT is a little over 50 miles from Aberdeen, the nearest major city. From modest beginnings, when a few portable tows were set up to take advantage of good snow cover, the centre has steadily expanded over the years. It is best suited to beginners and intermediates and is ideal for families. It has its own Race Training School which has proved to be a great success, with its pupils winning trophies abroad.

The first thing to strike you on arriving at the car park is that beginners have no distance at all to walk to the nursery slopes. The 100-seater café, the ski and board hire, ski school and equipment shop are all situated here, as is the ticket office. A fully computerised booking system allows skis and snowboards to be booked in advance, ensuring a faster service, especially for large groups. The Ski School offers instruction for all abilities, including snowboarding and race training; John Clark, the British Team coach, can often be seen putting his pupils through their paces, while his brother, Hugh, runs the Ski School, so instruction is of a high standard. A range of lift pass options is available and it is worth enquiring about special packages.

On the slopes, once first-timers have gained a little confidence, the beginners' tows are right there: the Robin, Wren, Petrel, Bunting and Ski School, all of which are green runs. For those moving to blue runs, there is a choice of three tows, offering a variety of gentle slopes, short steep sections and, quite often, well-formed moguls. Of these the Grouse is the longest, the Eagle the most popular and the Osprey the one which has a 200-metre dry slope, offering all-year skiing and snowboarding. Being laid on the natural contours of the hill, it is much more exciting than a conventional artificial slope. On the right hand side of the Eagle is a permanent race course, which can be used by the general public.

Moving on to red runs, the Falcon and Buzzard supply good potential for intermediates. The Falcon starts gently and increases in steepness as you descend. The moguls which form on this slope test the intermediate for flex and edge and, if worked hard enough, should considerably improve mogul techniques. The Buzzard is on the other side of the road (the A939) from the rest of the lifts and often has the best snow conditions – a must for the competent skier or snowboarder. The

THE LECHT

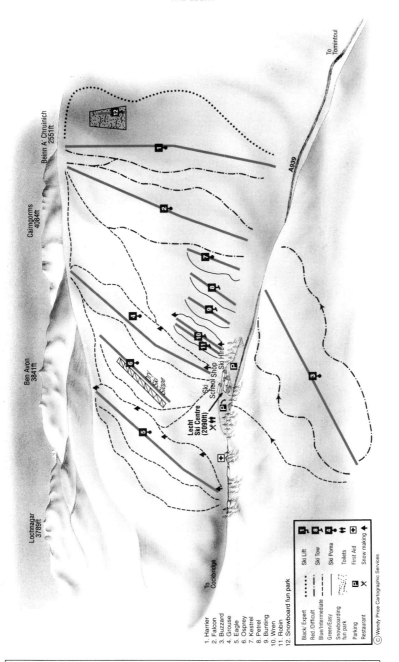

Key

1. Harrier
2. Falcon
3. Buzzard
4. Grouse
5. Eagle
6. Osprey
7. Kestrel
8. Petrel
9. Bunting
10. Wren
11. Robin
12. Snowboard fun park

Black/ Expert
Red/ Difficult
Blue/Intermediate
Green/Easy
Snowboarding fun park
Parking
Restaurant

Ski Lift
Ski Tow
Ski Poma
Toilets
First Aid
Snow making

© Wendy Price Cartographic Services

Belinn A' Chruinich 2551ft
Cairngorms 4084ft
Ben Avon 3841ft
Lochnagar 3789ft

To Tomintoul
A939
To Cockbridge

Lecht Ski Centre (2090ft)
Ski School Shop
Ski Hire
Dry Ski Slope

If you venture outside the designated ski-patrolled area, this is at your own risk. It is advised that you familiarise yourself with the boundaries before setting out by checking the large piste maps displayed at the centre.

The Lecht offers an ideal blend of family fun and excitement with beginners nursery slopes adjacent to the car park and a range of pistes to satisfy intermediate and advanced skiers and boarders.

- **New Snowboard Fun Park**
- **200m summer ski slope**
- **Snowmaking on most runs**
- **5 beginner, 3 intermediate and 3 advanced tows**
- **Equipment hire and tuition**

For more information on skiing in Grampian Highlands and to book accommodation, call 0990 39 33 39

For the latest SNOW CONDITIONS Report, visit our Web site – www.ski.scotland.net

LECHT
SKI COMPANY LTD

The Lecht Ski Company Ltd, Strathdon, Aberdeenshire AB36 8YP
Tel: 019756 51440
Fax: 019756 51426

final run of the system is the Harrier, which is the longest and steepest and is homologated by the F.I.S. for races up to National Slalom level, which speaks for itself.

All the runs are well-linked and very little walking is necessary. The latest modern technology to be installed here is the snow cannons which, when temperatures are low enough, can make snow on the Eagle, Grouse, Robin and Wren, allowing the season to start earlier and maintaining better snow cover throughout. On a cold winter's night the snow-making is a spectacular sight, and because the centre is conveniently situated beside the road, it can easily be viewed from the comfort of your car.

With the huge increase in demand for snowboarding facilities, a fun park has been created on the Harrier; the Lecht's half pipe cutter is the only one in Scotland, so keen shredders are well catered for. Although this resort is best suited to families and beginners, advanced skiers and riders should never forget that they are always learning, and the Lecht is the ideal centre for improving at all levels.

For more information, contact:

THE LECHT SKI CENTRE
Strathdon, Aberdeenshire AB36 8YP
Tel: 019756 51440
Fax: 019756 51426
Ski Hotline: 0891 654 657 (*Calls cost 50p per minute*)

Weather Conditions
Metcall Ski Scotland: 0336 411200

Accommodation Enquiries
Aberdeen & Grampian Tourist Board: 01330 825917
Aviemore Tourist Information Centre: 01479 810363;
Fax 01479 811063

General Tourist Enquiries
Braemar Tourist Information: 013397 41600;
Fax 013397 41643
Ceefax Page 591; Teletext Page 204

NEVIS RANGE

NEVIS RANGE is situated within ten minutes' drive of Fort William and is Scotland's highest snowsports centre, being on the flanks of Aonach Mor, which rises to 4,006 feet. It has a very modern lift system which includes a 2.3km six-person gondola for access to the hill and a quad chairlift. A double chairlift, the Braveheart, now extends the slopes over into the back corries (Coire Dubh) from the original Snowgoose area, opening up a large area of wilderness to skiers and snowboarders alike. Nevis Range has been the venue for Warren Miller's extreme ski and snowboarding filming. Cairngorm and Nevis Range were chosen against stiff competition to jointly host the European Cup Finals in March 1998 – a great coup!

The Base Station has a somewhat continental air, probably due to the ultra-modern gondola. Here there is a café, ski and snowboard equipment hire, ticket office, crêche and toilets. If you need hire and/or tuition, or would like a guide to help you explore the back corries, you should look at the many packages on offer – there are some good value options available.

The gondola takes you to the top station with its Snowgoose Restaurant, ski school meeting place, equipment shop, bar, first aid post and toilets. Looking up the hill, to the left is the beginners' area with its Lochy and Linnhe Button Tows and the Portable Trainer Tow. These gentle, well-pisted slopes are ideal for gaining confidence before tackling the next stage, the Alpha Button with its intermediate runs on either side.

One way to get up to the Goose and the Summit runs is to turn right out of the Gondola Station and head along the road to the Quad Chair. This whisks you swiftly up to the western boundary of the ski area. Leaving the chair to the right gives access to a good inter-mediate run. It also leads to one of the Snowboarding Fun Areas (the other is on Allt Sneachda, below the Goose T-bar). These offer such delights as log slides, table tops, barrel bonks, woop-de-doos or gap jumps. Leaving the chair to the left allows you to descend to the Goose T-bar, either by crossing the tow or by remaining on the Cats Alley side where the snow is often good. The Goose T-bar is a long one and takes you to the head of Snowgoose Gully. Wide, steep at the top (Duncan's Drop) and levelling out further down, this huge basin often

NEVIS RANGE

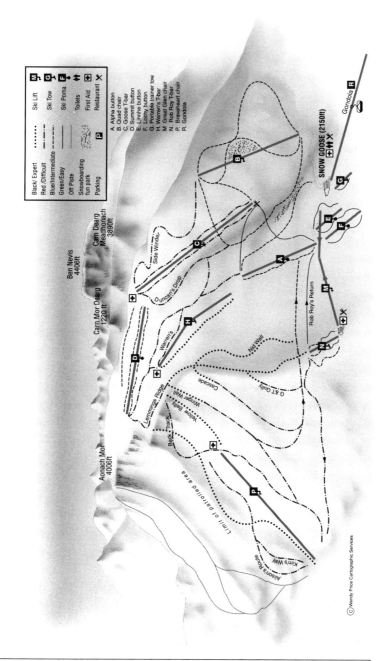

Legend:

⋯⋯	Black/ Expert	
– – –	Red /Difficult	
– · – · –	Blue/Intermediate	
— — —	Green/Easy	
░░░	Off Piste	
░░░	Snowboarding fun park	
P	Parking	

Ski Lift	Ski Tow	Ski Poma
Toilets	First Aid	Restaurant

A. Alpha button
B. Quad chair
C. Goose T-bar
D. Summit button
E. Linnhe button
F. Lochy button
G. Portable trainer tow
H. Warren's T-bar
M. Great Glen chair
N. Rob Roy T-bar
P. Braveheart chair
R. Gondola

Ben Nevis 4406ft
Carn Dearg Meadhonach 3890ft
Carn Mor Dearg 1220 ft
Aonach Mor 4006ft

Side Winder
Duncan's Drop
Warren's
Rob Roy's Return
Mid Wall
Cascade
G &T Gully
Yellow Belly
Winger Wall
Lemmings Ridge
Back Track
Kim's Way
Alison's Route
Limit of patrolled area

SNOW GOOSE (2150ft)
Gondola

© Wendy Price Cartographic Services

If you venture outside the designated ski-patrolled area, this is at your own risk. It is advised that you familiarise yourself with the boundaries before setting out by checking the large piste maps displayed at the centre.

Ski & Board
Nevis Range
Fort William, Scotland

Powder skiing "over the back" of Aonach Mor.

Scotland's Highest Ski Area

3 new lifts in 3 years • more extensive skiing • improved beginners' area

Nevis Range, Torlundy, Fort William   PH33 6SW.
Tel: 01397 705825. Website: www.ski.scotland.net

has good moguls, and its upper part is classed as a red run. Leaving the T-bar to the right gives access to the Side Winder and leads you back to the top of the Quad Chair.

From the top of the Goose T-bar you can reach the start of the Summit Tow, which must have one of the most spectacular views in Britain. By the time you reach the top, Ben Nevis dominates the scene and most ordinary mortals feel they just have to stand and absorb the vista for a while. To descend, intermediates should try the runs on either side of the tow, the Summit Run and Spider, while the more intrepid have a number of options. Look first for the open or closed signs, as prevailing snow and weather conditions dictate where skiing and snowboarding are possible – always respect the signs.

The most intrepid can try the aptly-named Chancer, a black run which plunges down into Coire Dubh, crossing the steep headwall below Climbers' Col before taking the direct route down to the start of the Braveheart Chairlift. This run is one of the great experiences of Scottish snowsports, wild and exhilarating and very taxing on the thigh muscles; not recommended for the first run of the day, or the last. Neither is Yellow Belly, in spite of its name. The Back Track provides a good long red route which snakes its way across the corrie and splits into Alison's Route and Kim's Way which join up again at the Braveheart Chair. Here too, the off-piste routes from the other back corries key into the lift system. If you want to explore these, guided tours are available – book at one of the ski school offices.

For a less heartstopping yet still demanding experience, coming off the Summit Tow you can opt to start off on Switch and then cut back to the Goose via the Upper Traverse, or use Switch or Lemming Ridge to reach the top of Warrens T-bar. The Warrens run itself is classed as difficult and always provides a variety of challenges. It leads back to the Lower Traverse, where you still have enough height to re-access the Goose T-Bar or Warrens T-bar.

From the top of Warrens you can reach many of the runs in Coire Dubh: Winger Wall, Cascade, G&T Gully, the Nid Ridge and the Nid Wall. The variations of route in this area are seemingly endless, and the potential for establishing your own favourites is its great attraction. By using the Rob Roy T-bar, with good snow cover you can ski back to the Snowgoose restaurant, or use the Great Glen chair. If you don't want to brave the entries to Coire Dubh described above, you can get to the Braveheart Chair from the top of the Rob Roy T-bar but this will involve a brisk uphill walk – very good for warming up the muscles!

The less fit may prefer to go back up Alpha and Warrens to reach the ridge again. The Rob Roy T-bar itself gives pleasant scope for beginners and intermediates on the Rob Roy, Blairs and Squiggle, with easy access to the area from the Great Glen Chairlift.

For information on Nevis Range contact:

NEVIS RANGE
Torlundy, Fort William, Inverness-shire PH33 6SW
Tel: 01397 705825/705855
Fax: 01397 705854

Web site: www.ski.scotland.net

Ski Hotline: 0891 654 660 (*Calls cost 50p per minute*)
Metcall Ski Scotland: 0331 411 200

Accommodation Enquiries:
Fort William Tourist Office, 01397 70378.

Some other books published by **LUATH** PRESS

WALK WITH LUATH
Mountain Days & Bothy Nights
Dave Brown and Ian Mitchell
ISBN 0 946487 15 4 PBK £7.50
Acknowledged as a classic of mountain writing still in demand ten years after its first publication, this book takes you into the bothies, howffs and dosses on the Scottish hills. Fishgut Mac, Desperate Dan and Stumpy the Big Yin stalk hill and public house, evading gamekeepers and Royalty with a camaraderie which was the trademark of Scots hillwalking in the early days.

'The fun element comes through ... how innocent the social polemic seems in our nastier world of today ... the book for the rucksack this year.'
Hamish Brown, SCOTTISH MOUNTAINEERING CLUB JOURNAL

'The doings, sayings, incongruities and idiosyncrasies of the denizens of the bothy underworld ... described in an easy philosophical style ... an authentic word picture of this part of the climbing scene in latter-day Scotland, which, like any good picture, will increase in charm over the years.'
Iain Smart, SCOTTISH MOUNTAINEERING CLUB JOURNAL

'The ideal book for nostalgic hillwalkers of the 60s, even just the armchair and public house variety ... humorous, entertaining, informative, written by two men with obvious expertise, knowledge and love of their subject.'
SCOTS INDEPENDENT

'Fifty years have made no difference. Your crowd is the one I used to know ... [This] must be the only complete dossers' guide ever put together.'
Alistair Borthwick, author of the immortal *Always a Little Further*.

The Joy of Hillwalking
Ralph Storer
ISBN 0 946487 28 6 PBK £6.95
Apart, perhaps, from the joy of sex, the joy of hillwalking brings more pleasure to more people than any other form of human activity.

'Alps, America, Scandinavia, you name it – Storer's been there, so why the hell shouldn't he bring all these various and varied places into his observations ... [He] even admits to losing his virginity after a day on the Aggy Ridge ... Well worth its place alongside Storer's earlier works.'
TAC

LUATH WALKING GUIDES
The highly respected and continually updated guides to the Cairngorms.

'Particularly good on local wildlife and how to see it'
THE COUNTRYMAN

Walks in the Cairngorms
Ernest Cross
ISBN 0 946487 09 X PBK £3.95
This selection of walks celebrates the rare birds, animals, plants and geological wonders of a region often believed difficult to penetrate on foot. Nothing is difficult with this guide in your pocket, as Cross gives a choice for every walker, and includes valuable tips on mountain safety and weather advice.
Ideal for walkers of all ages and skiers waiting for snowier skies.

Short Walks in the Cairngorms
Ernest Cross
ISBN 0 946487 23 5 PBK £3.95
Cross wrote this volume after overhearing a walker remark that there were no

LUATH PRESS LIMITED

Mountain Days
& Bothy Nights

TENTH ANNIVERSARY EDITION

DAVE BROWN & IAN MITCHELL

*'The fun element comes through...
how innocent the social polemic seems in
our nastier world of today... the book for
the rucksack this year.'*

Hamish Brown,
SMC JOURNAL

short walks for lazy ramblers in the Cairngorm region. Here is the answer: rambles through scenic woods with a welcoming pub at the end, birdwatching hints, glacier holes, or for the fit and ambitious, scrambles up hills to admire vistas of glorious scenery. Wildlife in the Cairngorms is unequalled elsewhere in Britain, and here it is brought to the binoculars of any walker who treads quietly and with respect.

LUATH GUIDES TO SCOTLAND

'Gentlemen, We have just returned from a six week stay in Scotland. I am convinced that Tom Atkinson is the best guidebook author I have ever read, about any place, any time.'
Edward Taylor, LOS ANGELES

These guides are not your traditional where-to-stay and what-to-eat books. They are companions in the rucksack or car seat, providing the discerning traveller with a blend of fiery opinion and moving description. Here you will find *'that curious pastiche of myths and legend and history that the Scots use to describe their heritage ... what battle happened in which glen between which clans; where the Picts sacrificed bulls as recently as the 17th century ... A lively counterpoint to the more standard, detached guidebook ... Intriguing.'*
THE WASHINGTON POST

These are perfect guides for the discerning visitor or resident to keep close by for reading again and again, written by authors who invite you to share their intimate knowledge and love of the areas covered.

South West Scotland

Tom Atkinson
ISBN 0 946487 04 9 PBK £4.95
This descriptive guide to the magical country of Robert Burns covers Kyle, Carrick, Galloway, Dumfries-shire, Kirkcudbrightshire and Wigtownshire. Hills, unknown moors and unspoiled beaches grace a land steeped in history and legend and portrayed with affection and deep delight.

An essential book for the visitor who yearns to feel at home in this land of peace and grandeur.

The Lonely Lands

Tom Atkinson
ISBN 0 946487 10 3 PBK £4.95
A guide to Inveraray, Glencoe, Loch Awe, Loch Lomond, Cowal, the Kyles of Bute and all of central Argyll written with insight, sympathy and loving detail. Once Atkinson has taken you there, these lands can never feel lonely. 'I have sought to make the complex simple, the beautiful accessible and the strange familiar,' he writes, and indeed he brings to the land a knowledge and affection only accessible to someone with intimate knowledge of the area. A must for travellers and natives who want to delve beneath the surface.

'Highly personal and somewhat quirky... steeped in the lore of Scotland.'
THE WASHINGTON POST

The Empty Lands

Tom Atkinson
ISBN 0 946487 13 8 PBK £4.95
The Highlands of Scotland from Ullapool to Bettyhill and Bonar Bridge to John O'Groats are landscapes of myth and legend, 'empty of people, but of nothing else that brings delight to any tired soul,' writes Atkinson. This highly personal guide describes Highland history and landscape with love, compassion and above all sheer magic. Essential reading for anyone who has dreamed of the Highlands.

Roads to the Isles

Tom Atkinson
ISBN 0 946487 01 4 PBK £4.95
Ardnamurchan, Morvern, Morar, Moidart and the west coast to Ullapool

LUATH PRESS LIMITED

Rum: Nature's Island

MAGNUS MAGNUSSON

are included in this guide to the Far West and Far North of Scotland. An unspoiled land of mountains, lochs and silver sands is brought to the walker's toe-tips (and to the reader's fingertips) in this stark, serene and evocative account of town, country and legend.

For any visitor to this Highland wonderland, Queen Victoria's favourite place on earth.

Highways and Byways in Mull and Iona

Peter Macnab

ISBN 0 946487 16 2 PBK £4.25

'The Isle of Mull is of Isles the fairest, Of ocean's gems 'tis the first and rarest.' So a local poet described it a hundred years ago, and this recently revised guide to Mull and sacred Iona, the most accessible islands of the Inner Hebrides, takes the reader on a delightful tour of these rare ocean gems, travelling with a native whose unparalleled knowledge and deep feeling for the area unlock the byways of the islands in all their natural beauty.

The Speyside Holiday Guide

Ernest Cross

ISBN 0 946487 27 8 PBK £4.95

Toothache in Tomintoul? Golf in Garmouth? Whatever your questions, Ernest Cross has the answers in this witty and knowledgeable guide to Speyside, one of Scotland's most popular holiday centres. A must for visitors and residents alike – there are still secrets to be discovered here!

NATURAL SCOTLAND

Rum: Nature's Island

Magnus Magnusson KBE

ISBN 0 946487 32 4 PBK £7.95

Rum: Nature's Island is the fascinating story of a Hebridean island from the earliest times through to the Clearances and its period as the sporting playground of a Lancashire industrial magnate, and on to its rebirth as a National Nature Re-

serve, a model for the active ecological management of Scotland's wild places.

Thoroughly researched and written in a lively accessible style, the book includes comprehensive coverage of the island's geology, animals and plants, and people, with a special chapter on the Edwardian extravaganza of Kinloch Castle. There is practical information for visitors to what was once known as 'the Forbidden Isle'; the book provides details of bothy and other accommodation, walks and nature trails. It closes with a positive vision for the island's future: biologically diverse, economically dynamic and ecologically sustainable.

Rum: Nature's Island is published in co-operation with Scottish Natural Heritage (of which Magnus Magnusson is Chairman) to mark the 40th anniversary of the acquistion of Rum by its predecessor, the Nature Conservancy.

SOCIAL HISTORY

The Crofting Years

Francis Thompson

ISBN 0 946487 06 5 PBK £6.95

Crofting is much more than a way of life. It is a storehouse of cultural, linguistic and moral values which holds together a scattered and struggling rural population. This book fills a blank in the written history of crofting over the last two centuries. Bloody conflicts and gunboat diplomacy, treachery, compassion, music and story: all figure in this mine of information on crofting in the Highlands and Islands of Scotland.

'I would recommend this book to all who are interested in the past, but even more so to those who are interested in the future survival of our way of life and culture.'
STORNOWAY GAZETTE

'A cleverly planned book ... the story told in simple words which compel attention ... [by] a Gaelic speaking

Lewisman with specialised knowledge of the crofting community.'
BOOKS IN SCOTLAND

'The book is a mine of information on many aspects of the past, among them the homes, the food, the music and the medicine of our crofting forebears.'
John M Macmillan, erstwhile CROFTERS COMMISSIONER FOR LEWIS AND HARRIS

'This fascinating book is recommended to anyone who has the interests of our language and culture at heart.'
Donnie Maclean, DIRECTOR OF AN COMUNN GAIDHEALACH, WESTERN ISLES

'Unlike many books on the subject, Crofting Years combines a radical political approach to Scottish crofting experience with a ruthless realism which while recognising the full tragedy and difficulty of his subject never descends to sentimentality or nostalgia.'
CHAPMAN

BIOGRAPHY

On the Trail of Robert Service

Wallace Lockhart
ISBN 0 946487 24 3 PBK £5.95
Known worldwide for his verses 'The Shooting of Dan McGrew' and 'The Cremation of Sam McGee', Service has woven his spell for Boy Scouts and learned professors alike. He chronicled the story of the Klondike Gold Rush, wandered the United States and Canada, Tahiti and Russia to become the bigger-than-life Bard of the Yukon. Whether you love or hate him, you can't ignore this cult figure. The book is a must for those who haven't yet met Robert Service.

'The story of a man who claimed that he wrote verse for those who wouldn't be seen dead reading poetry ... this enthralling biography will delight Service lovers in both the Old World and the New.'
SCOTS INDEPENDENT

Come Dungeons Dark

John Taylor Caldwell
ISBN 0 946487 19 7 PBK £6.95
Glasgow anarchist Guy Aldred died with 10p in his pocket in 1963 claiming there was better company in Barlinnie Prison than in the Corridors of Power. 'The Red Scourge' is remembered here by one who worked with him and spent 27 years as part of his turbulent household, sparring with Lenin, Sylvia Pankhurst and others as he struggled for freedom for his beloved fellow-man.

'The welcome and long-awaited biography of ... one of this country's most prolific radical propagandists ... Crank or visionary? ... whatever the verdict, the Glasgow anarchist has finally been given a fitting memorial.'
THE SCOTSMAN

Bare Feet and Tackety Boots

Archie Cameron
ISBN 0 946487 17 0 PBK £7.95
The island of Rhum before the First World War was the playground of its rich absentee landowner. A survivor of life a century gone tells his story. Factors and schoolmasters, midges and poaching, deer, ducks and MacBrayne's steamers: here social history and personal anecdote create a record of a way of life gone not long ago but already almost forgotten. This is the story the gentry couldn't tell.

'This book is an important piece of social history, for it gives an insight into how the other half lived in an era the likes of which will never be seen again.'
FORTHRIGHT MAGAZINE

'The authentic breath of the pawky, country-wise estate employee.'
THE OBSERVER

'Well observed and detailed account of island life in the early years of this century'
THE SCOTS MAGAZINE

'A very good read with the capacity to make the reader chuckle. A very talented writer.'
STORNOWAY GAZETTE

Seven Steps in the Dark

Bob Smith

ISBN 0 946487 21 9 PBK £8.95

'The story of his 45 years working at the faces of seven of Scotland's mines ... full of dignity and humanity ... unrivalled comradeship ... a vivid picture of mining life with all its heartbreaks and laughs.'
SCOTTISH MINER

Bob Smith went into the pit when he was fourteen years old to work with his father. They toiled in a low seam, just a few inches high, lying in the coal dust and mud, getting the coal out with pick and shovel. This is his story, but it is also the story of the last forty years of Scottish coalmining. A staunch Trades Unionist, one of those once described as "the enemy within", his life shows that in fact he has been dedicated utterly to the betterment of his fellow human beings.

HUMOUR/HISTORY

Revolting Scotland

Jeff Fallow

ISBN 0 946487 23 1 PBK £5.95

No Heiland Flings, tartan tams and kilty dolls in this witty and cutting cartoon history of bonnie Scotland frae the Ice Age tae Maggie Thatcher.

'An ideal gift for all Scottish teenagers.'
SCOTS INDEPENDENT

'The quality of the drawing [is] surely inspired by Japanese cartoonist Keiji Nakazawa whose books powerfully encapsulated the horror of Hiroshima ... refreshing to see a strong new medium like this.'
CHAPMAN

MUSIC AND DANCE

Highland Balls and Village Halls

Wallace Lockhart

ISBN 0 946487 12 X PBK £6.95

'Acknowledged as a classic in Scottish dancing circles throughout the world. Anecdotes, Scottish history, dress and dance steps are all included in this 'delightful little book, full of interest ... both a personal account and an understanding look at the making of traditions.'
NEW ZEALAND SCOTTISH COUNTRY DANCES MAGAZINE

'A delightful survey of Scottish dancing and custom. Informative, concise and opinionated, it guides the reader across the history and geography of country dance and ends by detailing the 12 dances every Scot should know – the most famous being the Eightsome Reel, "the greatest longest, rowdiest, most diabolically executed of all the Scottish country dances".'
THE HERALD

'A pot-pourri of every facet of Scottish country dancing. It will bring back memories of petronella turns and poussettes and make you eager to take part in a Broun's reel or a dashing white sergeant!'
DUNDEE COURIER AND ADVERTISER

'An excellent an very readable insight into the traditions and customs of Scottish country dancing. The author takes us on a tour from his own early days jigging in the village hall to the characters and traditions that have made our own brand of dance popular throughout the world.'
SUNDAY POST

LUATH PRESS LIMITED

The Supernatural Highlands

FRANCIS THOMPSON

POETRY

The Jolly Beggars or 'Love and Liberty'

Robert Burns

ISBN 0 946487 02 2 HB £8.00

Forgotten by the Bard himself, the rediscovery of this manuscript caused storms of acclaim at the turn of the 19th century. Yet it is hardly known today. It was set to music to form the only cantata ever written by Burns. SIR WALTER SCOTT wrote: 'Laid in the very lowest department of low life, the actors being a set of strolling vagrants ... extravagant glee and outrageous frolic ... not, perhaps, to be paralleled in the English language.' This edition is printed in Burns' own handwriting with an informative introduction by Tom Atkinson.

'The combination of facsimile, lively John Hampson graphics and provocative comment on the text makes for enjoyable reading.'
THE SCOTSMAN

Poems to be Read Aloud

selected and introduced by Tom Atkinson

ISBN 0 946487 00 6 PBK £5.00

This personal collection of doggerel and verse ranging from the tear-jerking 'Green Eye of the Yellow God' to the rarely-printed bawdy 'Eskimo Nell' has a lively cult following. Much borrowed and rarely returned, this is a book for reading aloud in very good company, preferably after a dram or twa. You are guaranteed a warm welcome if you arrive at a gathering with this little volume in your pocket.

'The essence is the audience.'
Tom Atkinson

FOLKLORE

The Supernatural Highlands

Francis Thompson

ISBN 0 946487 31 6 PBK £8.99

An authoritative exploration of the otherworld of the Highlander, happenings and beings hitherto thought to be outwith the ordinary forces of nature. A simple introduction to the way of life of rural Highland and Island communities, this new edition weaves a path through second sight, the evil eye, witchcraft, ghosts, fairies and other supernatural beings, offering new sight-lines on areas of belief once dismissed as folklore and supersition.

'Cool examination of the Highland folk tradition and the application to it of a systematic rationale. One cannot escape the impression in reading Mr Thompson's book that the sheer credulity of the Celts attracts dark prophecy like a magnet.'
PRESS AND JOURNAL

'Excellent guidebook to the Gaelic-speaking underworld.'
THE HERALD

Luath Press Limited
committed to publishing well written books worth reading

LUATH PRESS takes its name from Robert Burns, whose little collie Luath (*Gael.*, swift or nimble) tripped up Jean Armour at a wedding and gave him the chance to speak to the woman who was to be his wife and the abiding love of his life. Burns called one of *The Twa Dogs* Luath after Cuchullin's hunting dog in Ossian's *Fingal*. Luath Press grew up in the heart of Burns country, and now resides a few steps up the road from Burns' first lodgings in Edinburgh's Royal Mile.

Luath offers you distinctive writing with a hint of unexpected pleasures.

Most UK bookshops either carry our books in stock or can order them for you. To order direct from us, please send a £sterling cheque, postal order, international money order or your credit card details (number, address of cardholder and expiry date) to us at the address below. Please add post and packing as follows: UK – £1.00 per delivery address; overseas surface mail – £2.50 per delivery address; overseas airmail – £3.50 for the first book to each delivery address, plus £1.00 for each additional book by airmail to the same address. If your order is a gift, we will happily enclose your card or message at no extra charge.

Luath Press Limited
543/2 Castlehill
The Royal Mile
Edinburgh EH1 2ND
Telephone: 0131 225 4326
Fax: 0131 225 4324
email: gavin.macdougall@luath.co.uk
Website: www.luath.co.uk